Praise for *The Wild Wool S*

'The Wild Wool Shepherdess *reconnects us to our birthright as an integral part of the web of life. Full of authentic, bone-deep wisdom, this book reignites our sense of what's possible: affirms our core belief that we can reweave the pathways of the sacred and find meaning, purpose and our soul's path in the ways of the wild. Inspiring and intriguing in equal measure, this is a book for our times. Read it, and weave a new way of being into your life.'*

MANDA SCOTT, BESTSELLING AUTHOR OF
THE BOUDICA SERIES, PODCASTER AND TEACHER

'It is a rare gift to encounter an author who can touch the soul and awaken the heart with such power and authenticity. Elizabeth is one of those rare gifts. Her work is not just to be read, but to be lived, felt, and embodied.'

REBECCA CAMPBELL, BESTSELLING AUTHOR OF *LETTERS TO A STARSEED, LIGHT IS THE NEW BLACK, AND RISE SISTER RISE*

'Elizabeth's book is a beautifully woven delight, as she spins us into her personal journey of awakening and deepening, and her expansive vision of women's ancient mythology and sacred magic. We wander through the hills with her as she tends her sheep, then we dive with her into a spiritual journey that shakes her soul to its core.'

CAROLYN HILLYER, AUTHOR OF *THE WEAVERS' ORACLE, HER BONE BUNDLE, BOOK OF HAG* AND *SACRED HOUSE*

'I very nearly went to bed about two hours ago but something drew me to read… a little… and then I couldn't stop…. This book is tremendous: raw and wild and honest. Just read a few lines and see if you can stop!'

ROSAMUND YOUNG, BESTSELLING AUTHOR OF *THE SECRET LIFE OF COWS* AND *THE WISDOM OF SHEEP*

'The Wild Wool Shepherdess *is a primal call to awaken and align ourselves with nature and its cycles, advocating for a life deeply rooted in the rhythms of the Earth and body. This book is a rare gem, weaving hands-on practices and sharing the howl, hoot and bleat of the land and its animals. It relights old hilltop fires, sending out a beacon to those willing to remember.'*

NICOLE MASTERS, AUTHOR OF *FOR THE LOVE OF SOILS*

'I enjoyed reading, to feel the spiritual and physical work in Iekawehatie's (Elizabeth's adopted name) life is an endless cliff hanger. She walks the path of the okwaho, *the wolf, or path-maker in our language. A truly inspiring lifesaver who honours the ways of my people and every creature upon Mother Earth.'*

WAHIAKERON, 'APPLES ON THE GROUND', ELDER AND LANGUAGE KEEPER OF THE KANIENKEHA'KA NATION, KANAWAKE, TURTLE ISLAND

The
Wild Wool
Shepherdess

The
Wild Wool
Shepherdess

WEAVE THE ANCIENT PATH,
REIGNITE YOUR FEMININE FIRE

ELIZABETH KNEAFSEY

HAY HOUSE

Carlsbad, California • New York City
London • Sydney • New Delhi

Published in the United Kingdom by:
Hay House UK Ltd, The Sixth Floor, Watson House,
54 Baker Street, London W1U 7BU
Tel: +44 (0)20 3927 7290; www.hayhouse.co.uk

Published in the United States of America by:
Hay House LLC, PO Box 5100, Carlsbad, CA 92018-5100
Tel: (1) 760 431 7695 or (800) 654 5126; www.hayhouse.com

Published in Australia by:
Hay House Australia Publishing Pty Ltd, 18/36 Ralph St,
Alexandria NSW 2015
Tel: (61) 2 9669 4299; www.hayhouse.com.au

Published in India by:
Hay House Publishers (India) Pvt Ltd, Muskaan Complex,
Plot No.3, B-2, Vasant Kunj, New Delhi 110 070
Tel: (91) 11 4176 1620; www.hayhouse.co.in

Text © Elizabeth Kneafsey, 2024

The moral rights of the author have been asserted.

The information given in this book should not be treated as a substitute for professional medical advice; always consult a medical practitioner. Any use of information in this book is at the reader's discretion and risk. Neither the author nor the publisher can be held responsible for any loss, claim or damage arising out of the use, or misuse, of the suggestions made, the failure to take medical advice or for any material on third-party websites.

A catalogue record for this book is available from the British Library.

Tradepaper ISBN: 978-1-4019-7640-8
E-book ISBN: 978-1-83782-130-3
Audiobook ISBN: 978-1-83782-129-7

Interior illustrations: Meg Midwood

10 9 8 7 6 5 4 3 2 1

Printed in the United States of America

This product uses responsibly sourced papers and/or recycled materials. For more information, see www.hayhouse.com.

My gift to the world, Harry.

And to my ancestors for not letting me sleep.

Contents

List of Exercises

Introduction

'The two most important days of your life are the day
you were born and the day you find out why.'
Mark Twain

Like prey in the grips of a writhing crocodile in the final death throes of a kill, the battle is being lost; they know it, they sense the end. At the last point of evolutionary change within our human history, several thousands of years ago, there was a cataclysmic shift from the all-encompassing, nurturing power of the Chalice, where grandmothers and matrilineal law reigned, to the welding power of the Blade, where men implemented dominant rule, the power to take rather than give life and established oppressive control over humanity. We have lived under these conditions for too many years and now the cracks are widening. The truth seeps up like molten lava from the cracks in Mother Earth's surface. The Chalice is poking her head out from the gaping wounds inflicted on her by her so-called protectors; out from the trees, using birds to send messages. Any woman and man linked closely to their intuition will know exactly what I speak of, and their spirit has been waiting for a time such as this. If you are here reading this, it is by design; it has nothing to do with me. Voices are rising, tides are turning, women are empowering a new path and joining in co-operative partnership.

The dragons of ancient mythology are stirring from the underworld caves, some of them are already walking among us. I am writing this book in the (not coincidental) year of the dragon and this creature of folklore and fae stirs now in the souls of those who sense what lies ahead. They are awakening from their slumber, the stone chambers are crumbling away and chains are ripped from the walls for a time foretold such as this. Freedom beckons, the light is returning, the wind is howling, the air awaits.

How do we live in a world like this? How do we know the changes needed to be made in this world without elders to show us the way?

The answer, of our future, lies in our past.

My heart burns and aches for what we have lost. We should not only be empowering our daughters but emboldening our sons to stand alongside us. I am no guru, no awakened spiritual leader or enlightened healer who practises yoga daily while sipping on smoothies. I am a woman of the land with dirt in my nails and a quest in my heart.

Being a shepherdess and practitioner of ancient crafts is merely a fraction of who I am. What and who I truly am is something oppressed by today's society. I want to share this knowledge with you, so that you might recognize that which stirs your own soul.

'If you talk to the animals, they will talk to you
and you will know each other. If you do not talk

to them, you will not know them and what you do
not know, you fear. What one fears, one destroys.'
Chief Dan George

With strong roots and a clear vision, all paths from my heart outwards start here. They start from the council of the animal and plant nations, held up by the cosmos to return our mothers to their natural seat of authority, to bring back balance to our chaotic world. There is a path for women, calling us home. Back to our mother – Earth.

We, as a gender and human race, are in a state of emergency. Our ancestors and the faces beneath the Earth are so close now and relying on us, cheering us on. I see signs of them every day.

Yet, how do we fulfil this path and purpose in a success-fuelled, materialistic and money-driven patriarchal world? There is a way! And to find that, you must learn to live like a wolf among sheep. Become a modern-day warrior, paddling upstream, against the current and re-ignite Boudicca's spirit.

I invite you to step inside the canoe and paddle along on a journey with me through a landscape of tumultuous, mysterious and transformative stories interwoven with wool, ancient wisdom, sacred stones, a buffalo hide, love, blood, the drum, a wolf by my side and Grandmother Moon as my guide.

PART I

Remembering Our Roots

1

Now is the time to remember who we are, as life-givers, women. To look to our grandmothers, our ancestors, civilization throughout most of humanity. I walk on the precarious edge of the new and the old. I tell a story of a life carved out for me long ago, as it is for all of us, and how I found it not in the light guided by angels, but in the darkness of despair and devastation.

There is a feeling and sense at the moment that something has gone badly wrong in this world; we have forgotten the goddess that was worshipped for thousands of years and so we have forgotten ourselves. There was a time when women thrived, felt safe to roam in the world, were surrounded by protectors of their creation and didn't constantly have to prove themselves to partners, parents or society. To be a woman in today's world, we look to strangers behind screens for affirmation because the physical world sees us as worthless compared to a man's presence on the Earth. Let's not forget, we who live in the western world are privileged because we live a relatively free life, free from persecution every day. Fellow sisters living on the same planet as you and I encounter untold horrors just to survive. We are still seen across large swathes of the planet as second-class citizens, baby machines, sex toys, servants, slaves, inanimate objects to be abused, beaten, violated or paraded like trophies or trash.

To thrive, not merely survive, we must remember our roots. We are made of the moon and stardust and, therefore, we must remember how to connect daily with our spirit to survive this world, without everything spiralling out of control.

Across the planet something called 'God' has been used to support the denial, condemnation and mutilation of female sexuality for many years. Virtually all religious, cultural and political institutions stand on the erroneous concept that has been forced on us for centuries – that women are second to men. This concept reinforces the illusion that men exist to create the human world, whereas women exist to reproduce.

The dominant narrative pushed upon women, particularly our young impressionable girls, is that *sex* brings worthiness. It is beyond the time to start protecting our young children's minds from the idea that to get anywhere in life or to be liked, you need to *be sexy*. Share your body, sell it, shame it, sell your soul to the devil so long as it gets you noticed, right? We live in a world where young children and women are stolen from their parents' sides and sold on the black market as sex slaves in their precious young years. Forget all threats of World War III – that example, right there, is a very real danger to our youth. We should be more worried about this obsession with degrading young women than we are; instead we are *encouraging* it!

Mothers, fathers – we can show our daughters and sons that our bodies are sacred and precious and magically made, and we must protect them from predators lurking round every corner and honour them. Be bold and share physical beauty, but not for material or social profit. Women and girls can be sexy and do as they please for their own self-worth and love, as long as we teach them that their bodies are sacred and should be treated as such. The same with boys, who need to fully understand that they should treat girls with respect and take equal responsibility for contraception. All of this starts at home and spears out into the wider community. You're not supposed to be popular as a parent, but you are supposed to be present.

As well as the social need for this book to be written now, there are planetary reasons why this is the time for change. There has been a collapse and shift in our consciousness, which was also predicted by the planetary alignments. There had been an atmosphere of anticipation building at the turn of the millennium – of being on the precipice of a new era. On the winter solstice, 21 December 2020, we experienced the great conjunction of Jupiter and Saturn in Aquarius. This moved us from the influence of the element of earth to the element of air. I believe this is the threshold of a new era.

I am NOT an astrologer by any stretch, but I have a basic understanding of how influential the planetary movements and trajectories are in our physical lives and the knock-on effects of significant conjunctions (alignments) to our consciousness. In layman's terms, when Saturn and Jupiter come together, there is an intensity of old patterns dying and new fertility and growth taking shape. Saturn and Jupiter only conjunct at the start of a new decade, and for the last 200 years they have fallen in earth signs (particularly Taurus – my birth sign!). The big shift in 2020 herded these planets into the air signs, where they will stay until 2159. The symbol of the goddess in the air is the swan.

The winter solstice of 2020 saw the end of the earth element's influential focus on material security and resources. Now, the shift of not only Saturn and Jupiter but also Pluto into Aquarius for the next 20 years is set to bring disruption to established patriarchal order and centralized governmental systems. In this new aspect, the power returns to the people and brings huge, revolutionary changes in the way we communicate, innovate and dream. Change is happening at a rapid rate now and you will be feeling this internally, through your direction and life purpose, through your health and vision for the future.

In this section of the book, I reflect on my past and look to a future where women take a central place in the world. I talk of the animals that have so much to show us: the wolves, birds and my beloved sheep, now central to my life and livelihood. Follow my journey to inspire change in your life during this era of transformation.

CHAPTER 1

The Goddess Returning

L et us unearth the roots from which we emerge, looking back to a time when women were respected, looking at the wisdom of women and how their knowledge has shaped my path and this book. All of humanity was born through the pelvis of the woman – the life-giver. Once women were seen as the great givers of life and humanity and were revered as such, but there was a shift. Now the time has come when balance will be restored: the goddess is returning.

Men with grandmothers, sons of mothers, brothers who have sisters, fathers of daughters, uncles of nieces – nothing I speak of here, in uplifting women again, is to demote or degrade men. This process is about balance, and we could not live in a world without men, the 'life protectors' as they're called in Turtle Island (the name used for North America by Indigenous peoples). But the story of women must be told. For the past 5,000 years of patriarchal rule, men have tried to silence and oppress women, but the story of women – 'herstory' – tells us that for 30,000 years, god was seen as a woman. The only images of god from about 35,000 to 3,000BC were female.

Our ancient ancestors worshipped the fertile, life-giving Great Mother Goddess and we were born at this time in history to remind humanity of the original design of life on Earth.

Now is the time for women to return balance, order, truth and peace again. It is the reason I was born; it is my purpose to help every woman alive to remember who they are and to step up and answer our mother's call to go into battle. Women do not fight with swords, or ego or pride. We fight with the wisdom of the wolf, tenacity of the snake and strength of the oak – with knowledge that generations of men tried to burn from our memory. But men forget that a woman remembers everything with the steadfast resilience and power of a thousand goddesses.

But I didn't always think this way about women. From adolescence up until very recently, perhaps the last five years, I had a very low opinion of women and how I interacted with them. Women terrified me. I have been beaten, judged, mocked and shamed more harshly and with more hatred at the hands of women than by any man I've ever encountered – and endured more nefarious clashes with them. Most women I know have had the same experience. I shall tell you why and how to change your relationship to women and yourself in the coming pages.

The summer solstice is here as I write this now; the day is called Litha. On this day, we celebrate by bearing witness to the longest day and the shortest night. Solstice means 'the sun stands still' in Latin and the summer and winter solstices are my favourite days of the year. They're so magical and powerful, and our ancestors honoured them so much that they dedicated years of their lives to building huge monuments across the landscape to align the change in seasons with the cosmos in the most beautiful, powerful and structural ways.

When these monuments were being built about 5,000 years ago, women were the decision-makers of the community – the voices of authority – in certain parts of the globe. We need to understand how these past cultures, where women were revered, have been buried, denied and oppressed. And that starts with how these ideas and cultures were passed off as 'mythology' or 'primitive origins' by western male historians who insisted that true history started later: at the time when patriarchy really took hold.

I believe these huge structures were left as a reminder never to forget our origins from the Great Mother. No scholar or archaeologist knows their true meaning because information and knowledge were passed orally and physically in monuments and artefacts during this period. Today, we try to explain things so that they're rational to our limited consciousness. However, I, and many others, choose to believe in things we cannot explain, but that we feel and sense deep in our spirit and see with our third eye. The ancients foresaw the disbelieving times that we are living through, and the weight of the stones is so heavy no man can move them or change the message embedded in the core of the bedrock.

Stones stand out, like the goddess landscape voluptuously carved across the Wiltshire downs in England. Here, the Avebury stone circle represents the male and female form being in balance and cyclical unity down its avenue and throughout the perimeter stones. Nearby Silbury Hill represents the pregnant womb, surrounded by a moat of amniotic waters up the hill beyond towards the burial chamber, while West Kennet Long Barrow, abode of the dark mother, is where life begins in the darkness and ends in the same tomb.

Countless monuments were formed across the world in worship of the Great Mother, but I think that the most magical and powerful in the northern hemisphere is the landscape of Glastonbury Tor, or the Isle of Avalon, in Somerset, where blood well, or chalice well, sits within her perimeter of otherworldly death and rebirth energies.

Since these ancient times, to be a woman has come to mean being a thorn in the side of society. In the 1980s and 90s, when I grew up, I experienced this as feeling awkward, challenging and not as 'quiet' as I should have been. This era witnessed quite a radical change in the feminist movement. It was when Monica Sjöö, a heroine of mine, was writing *The Great Cosmic Mother* and *Spiral Journey*, two books that had a profound, life-changing impact on me. I believe that reading them started my upward journey to the place where I am now writing my own story about what it has been like to grow up in a male-dominated world. Although we are strides ahead of the times in which Monica grew up, I hope with all my heart that as you read this book, you will be filled with confidence and defiance at a world that still places you in a second class – with your worth based on looks rather than intelligence – and the wild magic you can bring to a desperate world.

Writing about patriarchal law in *The Great Cosmic Mother* (1987), Monica Sjöö and Barbara Mor called it a cynical legal system designed to uphold male power and control female energy. And, they added, while some men dominated others under these patriarchal systems, all men benefitted from their domination over the community of women.

My upbringing was in suburban working-class areas in the North and Midlands of England. It was the standard, male-fuelled experience where the lads got the opportunities, while the lasses made do with playing with dolls and baking cakes with mum. Ideas of bettering yourself were laughed at and mocked.

If you were good at anything and showed it, you risked bringing attention to yourself and that brought unwarranted abuse and bullying. I was naturally vibrant and rebellious in my younger years. I was a daredevil and if someone dared me to do something, I did it. Not to show off, but because I was being a kid – having fun; pushing boundaries.

Stuart, my best mate since I was four, once dared me to throw a huge rock into our neighbours' very expensive carp pond. Back then, aged 10, my mind didn't have the capacity to gauge risk or consequence, so I went ahead and enthusiastically launched the rock across the 1.8m (6ft) fence that had small gaps between the slats. 'SPLASH!' came the sound of impact, very swiftly followed by, 'Oi, you little bastards!' We didn't know that Sergeant Major (that was our name for him based on his stern demeanour) was in his garden and had seen the stone drop into his beloved fishpond, wreaking havoc among the lush lily pads and overpriced, prized pond life.

He gave chase; we didn't expect him to! Our legs didn't get the memo to run when he came storming out of the gate ready to rugby tackle us to the ground and give a us good whipping. Thankfully, he knew better than to beat the shit out of us, which was still an acceptable practice for your neighbours to do back then. Instead, after a very brief and pathetic chase, he marched us home to be reprimanded. Needless to say, he took us to my house, because in his words, 'She is the culprit.' I mean, of course it wasn't the angelic boy's fault. Must be that troublesome wild girl! A sentiment echoed countless times into my adulthood....

An hour later, comparing slipper marks across our backsides, we giggled it off and went on to plan our next attack. This time it involved a mask, running shoes and firecrackers!

I do feel bad years later, but at the time it was the most fun, hilarious, adrenaline-fuelled activity we could muster – as well as knock-a-door run! Did you ever do that? Flipping a coin to see who would be the knocker, the lookout and the pace-setter when running. I played it with Stuart and Justin, another childhood mate. I was a tomboy, and girls hated me for being pretty or good at sport, so I found comfort and acceptance with boys. Although that comfort doesn't last once you grow tits and they start to see you as a sex object in striped leggings, rather than an innocent girl desperate to be liked just for being herself.

At school, I was top of the class in sport and dance, but I don't recall a single experience when I was praised. Instead, I was hated and abused for this and for almost everything I was good at doing. This made me lose my confidence and desire to stand out, because they only brought me hardship and anxiety. My magic slowly faded and seeped into the cracks of the school playground. A precious childhood wasted as I sat for days on end staring out of the window wanting the pain to go away, wondering why I couldn't be out there playing on the grass field, picking daisies, instead of learning useless information I would never use in adult life. Meanwhile, I felt bits of white rubber being thrown in my hair by the two bullies behind me. 'Ha ha, she's got dandruff in her hair!', they shouted to a chorus of laughter. The teacher ignored their chants, and the ground did not swallow me up despite my internal pleas.

If you're weird, or good at anything or pretty, you're bullied. If you're quiet and keep your head down, you're bullied for being weak. There is no escape from this outdated institutional schooling system. Then, if your home life is equally unsettling, you build a fortress around yourself that no one can penetrate. Not only do you protect your spirit and light, but you also stop sharing yourself with the world and turn the dial to survival mode until you either take yourself out of this world, like many tragically do, or you hang on just long enough to be found again by the Great Cosmic Mother. She has been silently watching and waiting for you to return, dropping mythical breadcrumbs of hope along the journey for you to find. That recovery might take days, years, decades. It depends how well your defences were built.

Tragically, we don't support adolescent girls when they slip into a phase where their self-worth is low or non-existent – that's the dangerous point where they enter the world of sexual intimidation. Giving away their precious power in exchange for being wanted and liked, to get the attention they crave through sex.

But more tragic than this is that women learn to fight with each other to survive. Male dominance pits us against each other to be seen in this world and creates competition, so that instead of banding together and holding each other up through our trials, we rip each other apart, making us weak and keeping us in bondage to our oppressive past.

I could tell you countless stories of competition and betrayal by other women, and how deeply painful they have been. We've all been through this, where our greatest battles have been with other women through years of competition, mistrust and challenged self-worth. But none of us can turn back time in these instances of hurt. They are so deep and ingrained, reminiscent of the betrayal women were forced to use against each other in historic witch-hunt trials.

Betray or be killed. That trauma is embedded in our collective psyche and now we must spend the rest of our days trying to undo those scars on our lineage, so that we can teach our sons and daughters how to build a better world.

The way to change these ingrained patterns of behaviour begins at home, within your own spirit. The day I started to understand the weight of my own trauma and learn to love myself through it, was the day I saw women differently. I looked behind the mask of envy and jealousy and saw in each woman their soul trying to find their place in a world that doesn't freely accept our wild feminine power. We're all just young, impressionable girls with a wild nature, desperate for guidance, love and acceptance. We long for a gathering of grandmothers to sit us down, cup our cheeks with tenderness and kiss our foreheads with gentle reassurance. But they will also show us our mistakes and why we make them, and how to stop the tension between us in the fight to the top. Instead of standing on each other to reach the top, hold out your cupped hands for another woman to stand on and lift her to the top ahead of you. That is true fellowship of the feminine kind.

We are all different – we don't all understand and sympathize – but we should all care and love. As a woman, I am a grafter; I work outdoors, in the elements. I nurture and care for myself; I care for my boy. I am the provider, the hunter, the gatherer. I relish this role, but it has its challenges. Society craves restoration and balance between the masculine and feminine. The environment I work in – farming, country life – is brutal at times. You have to develop a thick skin as being undermined and belittled comes with the territory. It's not right and shouldn't continue, but it does. As a woman, I have learned to deal with the comments and show my strength or I would not last long. Simple.

Working out in the elements has also made me wonder why we are conditioned to fear the dark. Death and birth both happen in darkness. Many Celtic stories, myths and teachings have taught us that darkness is the sacred feminine and where our power lies, while daylight is masculine and where male power lies. All of humanity has been born from the dark womb of night into the light of the masculine day, then we return to the cave and darkness, back to our mother land when we die. But we have been coerced to fear darkness by a patriarchal society that has tried to erase women and women's power over the last 5,000 years.

> *'When women work on reclaiming the lost*
> *part of themselves, they're also working on*
> *reclaiming the lost soul of the culture.'*
> **Maureen Murdock**

The solstice has always been a time of yearly death and rebirth. Our ancestors knew the importance of death and left us messages to remind us in the form of stone circles and burial chambers. Since humanity has lost its way, the only compass we have to remember who we are and how to navigate this journey of life is to look back to their teaching and ceremonies. How often have you marked the occasion of the solstice, equinox or Samhain? When I understood about the importance of marking these seasonal occasions and portal points of change and renewal, I delved deep into embracing these old traditions because they align us with our true nature. When you align with your true nature, your whole life will change – it did with me. The internal feminine flame is reignited.

So, don't let these moments pass you by this year. Light a candle and live just by that light, or make a fire and think about all the things that have happened to you this year. What will you burn that no longer serves you? What will you keep and be grateful for? Leave offerings for your ancestors, such as feathers, bundles of herbs or food; sing their songs; tell their stories. Go out into the dark and walk beneath the stars; do it alone. Feel the fear and do it anyway and wait for your eyes to open and see the stars like you've never seen them before. Love wholly and live truly; heal conflict and repair lost relationships with loved ones or yourself (most importantly, yourself). Simply being alive and being you, *that* is honouring your ancestors and feminine dark power.

CHAPTER 2

The Life-Giver

I now see women as the most incredible force of nature on Earth.
During the reign of Boudicca, the ancient British queen of the Iceni
tribe circa AD60–61, there was an uprising like we've never seen
before or since. Both men and women followed her with passion
and loyalty into battle – a historic uprising by the native Celtic
Britons against the male-dominated Roman regime. Imagine telling
that story to the grandkids!

> *'Whether she is seen as the benevolent Mother of All
> Living, or the Goddess of bloody battle, or the Death
> Goddess, or the prophetic witch – the attitude toward
> life in matriarchal society remains the same. All life is
> created out of the Mother and is one with her.'*
>
> **Monica Sjöö**

I crave a grandmother, an elder, a role model who has walked
through the fires of life. Someone to sit with me at the hearth of
both daily life and dreamworlds as I receive my visions; a wise
woman to help interpret what I see. A woman who will open her

wings like an eagle and shelter me from the storms, through times of turmoil or indecision, but who will also force me to stand out in the storm, sodden and exposed, stripped bare and vulnerable until I've endured the lesson meant for me. It is like a tale from days long gone, but I crave the return of them.

Maybe we won't see the full return of the life-giver's world – the women who walk with wolves and dwell among the trees raising children made of steel, and who understand circadian rhythms as well as computer game formulas. But you can be the seed; you can be a mentor; you can be that vision you want to see in the world. Imagine what it would be like having a tribe of women behind you, supporting you.

Circles create a space for us to stop and breathe. They offer a chance to ask yourself 'How am I doing, really?' They are where you can be held by your sisters when the answer comes. This is the time to speak out our dreams, manifest them in fire and ceremony. Remembering a time when we held in deep reverence our gift of life-giving, we are filled with a magical universe inside our belly. Even if we have no children, through choice or the grief of being unable to birth a physical child into the world, still know that we are life-givers from birth, not life-takers, and our voice and energy are important in this world.

Celebrate your uniqueness, share challenges, set intentions. We don't need science and studies to tell us that when we form close bonds with other women, it increases our health and happiness. Our ancestors relied on each other for survival. We raised each other's children, cared for each other's parents when they were sick, cooked together, mourned together, gave birth to miracles together. We supported each other through every trial and triumph unlike our independent, disconnected, comfortable lives today, where we shut

Time to dig deep, warrior up, unshackle your thoughts, embrace your sensuality, paint your body in victory, dance beneath the moonlight, bathe in the stardust and run with the wolves.

ourselves behind brick walls and think no one cares enough to carry our pain. But when women connect under a full moon and forest, magic happens. The power in these moments is life changing....

I have never lived in these supportive communities, but I have witnessed them through my female line. I feel it in my core, I've witnessed it in tribal nations and Indigenous cultures. Depression, insecurity, loneliness and anxiety are symptoms of our modern-day comforts, which tear apart our connections to nature and our tribal sisters.

Now is the time to unravel your conditioning. It's the time to discover your ancestral lineage and awaken from the slumber we put ourselves in based on the limitations society places on us. Time to dig deep, warrior up, unshackle your thoughts, embrace your sensuality, paint your body in victory, dance beneath the moonlight, bathe in the stardust and run with the wolves.

There's a dream I have, one that I feel my whole life has been on a path towards. A dream built on the foundations of hope and the rebirth of a new world. But the dream is just out of my reach – it's on the other side of the bridge in front of me. This bridge is covered in thorns and barbed wire, glass and fire. I can see the dream in all its glory. I can hear the voices and songs echoing from the other side. I can see the women gathering and beating the drums, calling in those who should come. As I look for a way across, all routes are blocked, or treacherous and uncertain. I can see but I cannot be a part of the dream.

Why does this happen? Why are there obstacles? They are not made of nature but of mankind.

If reading this is stirring emotions in you, or raising questions you want to ask or need answering, may I encourage you to create a space for yourself in your home where you can focus your mind. I'd like you to build an altar of things that are precious to you: stones, jewellery, pictures, incense. Now perform a ceremony to call out your sacred truth and drag it from the depths of the dream world into the living embodiment of who you really are and can become. To do this, use a smudge stick, or make one of mugwort or sage and pine. Use any combination available to you. Smudging is a sacred practice used historically across my land and by many Indigenous cultures worldwide. Please be mindful of which sacred plants you use, make your own bundles with herbs local to your area, or source them from Indigenous-owned companies.

AWAKENING CEREMONY
USING A SMUDGE STICK

To make a smudge stick, gather the plants. Identify and collect mugwort, which grows wild in areas of waste lands, farmland hedgerows and woodland perimeters. Magical mugwort has three wonderful qualities, it:

◊ increases your senses, intuition and communication with your spirit and the otherworld

◊ helps you understand, translate and decode any messages you may receive within your dreamworld

◊ grounds you back in the physical realm, so that you can weave all you have learned from the messages received and integrate them back into your physical life.

You can also use pine needles or cedar branches and sage of any variety in the following ceremony.

1. Hang up the plants in your kitchen for a day or two to dry a little.

2. Then, before they are completely dry, start to gather pieces to create a long bunch, about a hand-length long and the thickness of an apricot. Squeeze them together and wrap with either thin cotton or twine along the length of the bunch, working from the bottom to the top and pulling all leaves and needles in so they're trapped by the cotton. This ensures that the smudge stick won't fall apart when burned. Tie off the cotton at the base and leave the stick hanging somewhere to dry for a week or two.

3. When you're ready to begin, go to the altar with your smudge stick, light one end and let the flame take hold for a few seconds.

4. Blow it out and place it in a dry bowl to gently smoke away. This sends the aroma and swirls of smoky energy into the air and your lungs, feeding your spirit with the medicine of the earth. There lies the magic realm and the place of shapeshifters, storytellers, selkies and swans.

5. Light your smudge stick again and blow the smoke into the air and move the stick in an anticlockwise direction – the direction the heart pumps blood around your body. Anticlockwise is also the direction of growth in nature that aligns with Mother Earth's DNA. The clockwise direction is patriarchal, so with each coil on the matriarchal direction you are undoing this conditioning.

6. Then, continue to circle your body twice above your heart and twice below, making sure you cover your hair in the smoke. This process cleanses you and carries away your intentions to the eagles.

7. Lastly, wave the smoke with your hand or a feather to your eyes, your heart (pressing here), then your belly and then your womb.

◇◇◇◇◇◇◇◇◇◇◇◇◇◇◇◇◇◇

CHAPTER 3

Fire

F ire is both an ancient, human-made tool and a sacred, natural
element. It symbolizes the deep strength and passion hiding
deeply within us all and the full force of nature.

Fire in the Belly

We bury the fire in our bellies in order to survive and fit in;
to be loved, liked and wanted. We put our needs and desire for
affirmation on others. There are so few true elders left to show us the
way. Each death of an elder leaves a crack in the rock of the earth
where, without their wisdom being passed on, all that knowledge
disappears, to be re-consumed by the Mother.

My older sister is an avid reader. There is always a book in her
hand. I was envious of her ability to be enthralled by reading. I
really wanted to be that 'intelligent type' who could keep their
concentration long enough to read a whole book, a chapter even,
without being distracted. But I was too wild and untamed. I wanted
to be out with my pal Stuart picking ball bearings out of the cracks

in the pavements, chasing butterflies and trying to catch them, and running up the back field throwing balls at each other. We also bloody loved jumping out of a dead tree into a haystack mound we'd built at the bottom. We took turns climbing up and leaping what must have been 3m (10ft) into the mound of hay below.

The hay was stolen from a freshly cut wheat field, much to the farmer's annoyance. When I look back now, I realize (especially now that I'm a farmer myself – the irony!) what a royal pain in the arse we must have been to him. We made a game of him getting so pissed off at us for messing with the straw so that he'd stop mid-tedding (turning the hay), leap out of his tractor, engine running, and give chase to a hoard of screeching kids as we scattered and fled to all four corners of the village to get away from him. The adrenaline was real! I remember one time, he chased Stuart and me. We bolted down the jitty and hopped over a neighbour's brick wall, crouching down and leaning on each other's shoulders, shushing each other and holding our breath as his heavy footsteps came sprinting past. The relief as we heard him disappear around the corner was huge. I might have even peed myself on the odd occasion when the excitement of the chase intensified. Happy days.

There was a particular collection of books I was obsessed with in my adolescence. I realize they're not Jane Austen, but they gave me the nudge I needed inside to affirm my feelings of joy and wonder at being a kid and how to play. They were the *Beano* and *Dandy* annuals. Every Christmas, my parents would buy me the latest edition and into the stocking it would go. I couldn't tear myself away from those books. I still have them in the loft somewhere. My favourite character was Beryl the Peril. Her name says it all and I'm sure I dreamed myself into the storyline of that character many times. She was a girl who was always in trouble. She was a rebel, always sticking two fingers up at the bullies with fearless disdain. Never one to be told what to do, she also didn't deal well with school. We were birds of a feather; I was the living version of this fictional character – daring, brash, sensitive and wild.

Enid Blyton was another escape for me. Her endless tales of running away on adventures, *The Magic Faraway Tree* and *The Famous Five* were the script for a childhood I dreamed about. Carefree summer days spent with dogs and friends making memories that would turn into real-life storybooks. Enid was a proper laugh, wasn't she? She must have been taking the piss when she called her main characters 'Dick' and 'Fanny'! I'd always chuckle to myself when I was reading them to my son when he was a child. Maybe we've lost the childlike innocence of past generations. It's our modern warped minds that find that sort of thing sexual, funny or embarrassing because it's been rammed down our throat in the western world.

I wonder how this generation will cope when our grandparents are gone and we haven't cared enough, or sat long enough, to listen to their wisdom or learned their skills and knowledge. Once it's gone, it's gone. An African proverb says that when an elder dies, it's like a library going up in flames.

If your grandparents and parents are still on this Earth, go and sit with them. Ask them about their lives, what they've learned, what's important, what their best story is, what their most valuable piece of life advice is and what they want to be remembered for. Record it, write it down, film it. No one ever regrets doing this when they're gone, you're likely to regret not doing it once your loved ones are gone and it's too late.

The generation who grafted for a living is slipping away. Very few alive in the world now understand a hard day's work because they see that applying make-up on a social-media platform gets you more money and status than building your own house, or learning how to become a carpenter, tan a hide or mend a car. We owe it to the younger ones to show them the way of our grandparents and great grandparents. Our generation is at a pivotal point in history; like the old-fashioned scales, where you add metal weights on one side and an object on the other, they can tip in either direction. We are the cogs that will determine the course of humanity – no wonder our anxiety levels are through the roof! You may not want to carry such a burden, and I wish our ancestors hadn't placed such a responsibility on our shoulders, but we are born now for a task such as this. You could look at that as a privilege. We have a choice – will you take up the baton? Will you light the beacon for humanity and fight for our children? What does that fight even look like?

'Always be prepared' is a motto of mine. In my daily rounds, I just can't go anywhere without a flask of tea 'just in case' – just in case the apocalypse happens on the way to Lidl, right? Most of my truck journeys involve a flask, a snack bag and a wool blanket.

Live with the mentality that 'it might happen' rather than 'I wish I'd been more prepared'.

My theory is based on a question. Ask yourself: Can you survive in this world without modern-day luxuries and can you teach others how to empower themselves and their families with vital life-sustaining skills? If you answer 'no', I can help you make a start down a path that your grandkids and future loved ones will be thankful that you followed. Because it's not a matter of IF you need these skills, it's WHEN.

Can you or have you ever grown your own food?

You can do this even if you live in a tower block with no garden. Try tomatoes in pots, salad leaves in a windowsill box, potatoes in hessian bags on the balcony or patio. If you have a garden, section off an area and throw in a few seeds. You'll not only feed your family but an abundance of wildlife that will come and pollenate your plants. Start small and, before you know it, you will love the feeling of going out into the garden and harvesting your own organic, pesticide-free produce so much that you'll plant more each year and may even take on an allotment. Maybe you could contact a local farmer or parish council to see if you can rent a small plot to grow food for your local community? This leads to the 'share' mentality. There is no better feeling than swapping produce and goods between your neighbours and wider community. That's what we should be working towards. It makes you feel less 'me and them' and more 'us' as fellow humans.

Have you ever raised your own meat to eat?

I mean proper meat, not modern mass-produced meat that may upset our delicate guts due to the chemicals in animal feed, or the fact that our soil has become so depleted of minerals and organic matter that our animals are undernourished. If you buy your meat, aim to support small family-run farms and artisan organic smallholders, like me. But raising your own animals is not as daunting as it seems – a small flock of sheep, a couple of pigs, chickens and ducks can easily be accommodated in a back garden. You need to research the legal requirements regarding keeping livestock and research the kind of animals you'd like to raise. If it's sheep, there are two great books I swear by: *Natural Sheep Care* by Pat Coleby and *The Complete Herbal Handbook for Farm and Stable* by Juliette De Baïracli Levy.

In addition, read any books by Rosamund Young. Also consider volunteering at local farms to get hands-on experience, or go on an animal-husbandry course like the ones I run, which teach you how to raise sheep, use the whole animal and honour them through their life and death.

Have you ever hunted, skinned and butchered an animal to eat – whether they were roadkill, domestic stock or game birds?

There are some great places that run courses on these subjects in the UK and I teach these skills on my retreats. I cannot stress enough how valuable these skills are, but they are so underrated in a world where food comes ready packaged in plastic.

Do you know how to make fire from scratch with no lighter, matches or other fuel source?

I explain one of these methods later in the book (*see page 37*), and you can also look at videos on YouTube to expand your knowledge. Being able to light a fire is not only a great party trick and a good way to impress your mates, it can also save your life. No joke!

Do you know how to keep yourself and your family warm and clothed without modern-day technologies?

Consider using ancient practices, such as tanning sheepskins and deer hides, instead of buying mass-produced, chemically made products for your home, and create environmentally friendly, sustainable, handmade items with locally sourced wool and fibres. Not only are these key skills to pass on to your children, but it's incredibly empowering to be able to be self-sufficient.

We can survive fully off-grid on renewable materials and foraged food. We lived like this for thousands of years and although I recognize that our ancestors would be envious of the luxuries we have today, such as hot water and central heating, they've become a crutch to take us away from our true nature. The reason so many of us feel lost in this world is because it's so damn hard and depressing to live in a world that prioritizes convenience. It sounds counterintuitive, but the easy, lazy life is mind-numbing and demoralising. We are made of actual stardust and our souls only recognize the wild and being out in the elements. Why do you think we automatically feel better when we go there, out in nature to see a sunset, breathe in freshly cut grass or hear the trickle of running water? The longer we continue to live separate lives inside concrete houses, away from the soil and sand beneath our fingers and toes, the more we ebb away into extinction.

Somewhere in our not-too-distant ancestry, we were all born of a tribe.

This tribe of people loved the Earth and worked alongside her. They nurtured her, sacrificed their blood over her, worshipped and protected her. Through time and history this tribe – our ancestors – became infected by a new, more disturbing and disconnected world and way of living. If you perceive glimpses of the ways of this original tribe in your life now, hold on to them fiercely. Hold on to the old ways, the pure and gentle ways, so that every generation to come will be offered the chance to restore our world. For, if the old ways are lost, we are also lost.

Fire in the Heart

Although I have good memories of childhood, those years were often full of angst and confusion – in my mind and in my physical world. Childhood was a place where my magic was misunderstood, oppressed and challenged as an 'issue', an annoyance or a negative trait, and people labelled me 'the weird kid'.

I know, looking back, that during my adolescence, my mother struggled to communicate with me. For a young child, I was intense and deep and would go into moods where I would mute myself, hide away from everyone and seek solace in the fields and woods nestled around the fairly average, working-class estate where we lived in a lovely little rural village on the outskirts of Nottingham. The only thing in my life that didn't require me to explain what was wrong with me was my dog Jodie. She just accepted me, stayed with me and loved me unconditionally. I would often be found out in the shed where she slept and we would be chatting away. When I say we, I mean she mostly listened to my teenage torment without much choice in the matter – poor soul!

One day, I was beaten up quite badly at school by two girls who didn't like my ability to run faster than them. Home was no refuge, with conflict over supper between parents going through a separation. That night there was a huge thunderstorm, so out I crept to the shed where Jodie and our new German shepherd pup slept. Jodie was sitting in her wooden whelping box, tail beating and eyes beaming as I entered. I sat next to her and squeezed her to make sure she was okay in the thunder. My tears dripped onto her fox-red golden fur. She licked at the saltiness on my cheek and trembled as the storm clouds passed overhead. It was a powerful moment that shaped my life.

Hold on to the old ways, the pure and gentle ways, so that every generation to come will be offered the chance to restore our world. For, if the old ways are lost, we are also lost.

Why do I remember it so well and vividly? Was it because the thunder was a warning to me to take the dogs inside? Or, was it because of what came after...? It's so much more poignant now, remembering that moment, because that would have been one of the last times I had with her. A few days later, Jodie and my German shepherd pup were stolen from their shed in the garden and never seen again. They disappeared without trace.

For months, I waited by our garden gate and searched the local fields where we would go running together. I'd hoped she'd go out searching for me. We used to go running together when I was training for the school cross-country championships, and there was only one time in all her nine years that I left her at home. We took the same route every day, which was around 5km (3 miles) up to the old Roman encampment woods, Fox Wood, along the ridge and back down through the park and across the cricket fields towards home. That one time, when I was coming down Bonner Hill, a steep slope banked by an ancient hedgerow and barley fields to the right, I saw her – the golden labrador that should have been at home. She was halfway down the hill waiting for me. As I got closer, she bounded about in excitement and I swear if she could have talked, she would have muttered 'Why the hell did you go without me?' My heart broke a little in that moment and I never left her at home again. We were constant companions. So, when I went outside that summer morning to open their kennel, I never expected to see an empty box and bed, never to see Jodie's beautiful face again, never to say goodbye or tell her I'll find her and always remember her.

I was utterly heartbroken and lost. I stared out of my bedroom window every day after school, desperate to see her ambling up the road. I badgered my mum weekly to call the local RSPCA or dog pound, put adverts in papers, keep searching. Jodie would be terrified without her family; my brother, sisters and I were all she'd ever known. Months went by, then years... and nothing. It was as though she had never existed.

When someone or an animal you love dies, it's final; you know their destination. But when someone is missing, you're forever searching for closure, an end point, a conclusion. It never came.

I look back now, and it still grieves me; I am writing through the tears. But I have the wisdom now to know that Jodie was most likely an angel. A guardian, sent for just a short while to hold me through some of the hardest days of my life. Because the Great Spirit knows me intimately and will send exactly what's needed in my life, at exactly the right time, to see me through. You might not know why a guardian comes, who or what they are, or how long they'll stay, but they come to be a part of your destiny, a chapter in your story. Jodie is one of the first things I write about because it was at this point in my life that I knew my heart was formed with the blood of the animal spirits, and I was destined to live alongside them.

As a young girl with very heightened senses, I would have many visions and dreams, many that I simply did not understand or had no guidance to interpret.

I would lie awake in bed at night and blow my dreams and prayers up to God/The Great Spirit/Mother Earth, hoping she'd receive them and reveal the answers... until she showed me that I don't always need to look up to find a living spirit in everything. I wanted to express myself and live in the way the native cultures of the world did, with the purest connection to nature ever found.

Then, through suffering, circumstance and wounds, I just began to push everything I loved incredibly deep.

My lineage is formed, historically, of predominantly Irish and Scandinavian blood. Somewhere in my DNA and heritage I am born of an ancient tribe. A tribe who adored and respected and lived in harmony with the Earth, seas, fire and wind. My senses are intense and alert daily to my surroundings and encounters. Sometimes these senses are so overloaded by this fast-paced, high-intensity society that I am left drained and unable to cope well with even the most monotonous of tasks.

I believe this sensitivity stems from a time when we were all in tune with nature and the simplicity of connection, with animals, the elements and the landscape, living a life of harmony.

Harmony is something we know little of in the western world. It is an ideology, a conscious state that we have little desire for in a world where what makes up our daily rituals are work, consumerism, anger, frustration, depression, lack of contentment and a void that is so tangible, we scarcely dare think about, or consider, challenging it. The weight of oppression in our society and daily life sucks out the core of our true selves. I speak of my own experience here, but many people I encounter on a daily basis suffer in the same way. You can see it in their eyes, in my eyes.

A lady I once worked for remarked to me: 'You are a good soul Elizabeth, but there's a real sadness in your eyes.'

I shall tell you where this sadness comes from. It is not sadness caused from childhood trauma, although we were all exposed to elements of this. It is not born of learned behaviour or conditioning, although we have to fight daily to fend off this unhappy state and the bitterness that threatens to consume the spirit. It is also not from broken relationships or abandonment, although I have experienced both and loathed myself because of guilt and shame.

For me, and maybe you, the sadness is because I don't belong here. My body and mind are tortured because I can't go back in time. I can't sit with that child many centuries ago, who ran through the glades and meadows of the wilderness, free to roam; made food from foraging, pelts from animals we respected and hunted; sat around fires and shared stories of brave warriors and wise women; brought healing to the wounded. I can't learn from great teachers, medicine men and women who used the life force of energy to ask the Great Spirit for wisdom and enlightenment. I can't make baskets, beaded jewellery or clothing, sit quietly, calmly, burning herbs, telling stories, laughing and nurturing each other's souls with my sisters and elders.

Everyone would say that I was deep; they couldn't read me. I would never say how I was feeling for fear of being seen as weird. I simply didn't fit into my Midlands, working-class, council-estate roots. It did come out at times, in small ways: the music I listened to, the dancing, the clothes I wore, the jewellery I loved and collected and still have.

Through my early years and into adolescence, the fire was lit, ignited and burned so strongly and brightly in my spirit, until I started suffocating and burying the fire to try to survive and fit in. We all do this, to be loved, liked and wanted – put our needs and desire for affirmation on others. But no matter the bond or love between you, it is not their burden to carry or wound to heal. Only you can do that, but we are duped into believing that the knight in shining armour will be our saviour... the one who will kiss all the cracks and smother them over with plasters. But plasters break and rot and fall away and the cracks are still there when the time comes to heal.

When we do not know where to put our angst, we fall into patterns of self-harm. Children no longer walk through life alongside their elders to gain skills and confidence in their gifts and wisdom. Those traditions are lost to TV and social media in an age of cynicism, shallow, lazy parenting and the loss of community.

Fire of the Earth

Fire doesn't only exist in our bellies and hearts – fire is also sacred, the element of human survival. Women are the builders of the camp and hearth; we need to relearn skills to survive what lies ahead. Start with fire: learn how to source materials in the wild, build it, shelter it and cook over it.

The ancient art of fire-making

Every night after a full day during lambing season, I'd make a fire and cook my dinner. This practice is something I've always loved. It takes me back a thousand years to a place where my ancestors lived.

I don't just make fire to eat, I make fire to heal the scars of the day. Fire is so much more than warmth and provision. It's spirit, ceremony and healing. Yes, I know there are fancy things like matches and lighters available nowadays, but I like to make my life difficult – alright!

MAKING A FIRE

Fire can be created through friction by rapidly grinding pieces of solid combustible material (such as wood) against each other, which are heated and create an ember. But one of the easiest match-free ways to start a fire is to use flint and steel. Flint and steel kits can be purchased relatively inexpensively and are easy to use if you also have a tinder kit, especially if your tinder kit includes char cloth.

Flint is a hard grey rock occurring predominantly on landscapes of chalk or limestone. Flint has been used to make stone tools and start fires for more than 3 million years. Flint breaks into different sized chips with sharp edges through a process known as flint-knapping. When struck against steel, flint produces a large amount of spark to light the correct tinder.

Tinder can be found in the wild as dry grass, birch bark, dry moss, dry lichen or cedar bark (the inner pith) or around the modern home as newspaper, cotton wool or char cloth.

Char cloth is simply linen or cotton cloth (such as an old ripped-up t-shirt) that has been burned in a low-oxygen environment. I use a small metal tin with a lid, such as an old biscuit tin. Make a small hole in the top to allow the smoke and pressure to escape. Pack the tin with the cloth, which has been cut into 6cm (2.5in) square pieces. Then place the tin on some hot coals in a fire for around 20 minutes or until the smoke subsides through the hole in the top of the tin. Leave it to cool overnight and in the morning, you will have perfect, black char cloth ready to take a flame and burn to a cinder.

A good piece of steel may be in a 'c' shape that fits around the hand; these can be purchased as 'fire steels' online . Or there are 'u' shaped steels for folk with larger hands.

Now you have your tools, here's how to start the fire:

1. Prepare your fire bed of tinder, kindling and wood and lay a few pieces of char cloth on top.

2. Take a piece of flint, about 8cm (3in) by 6cm (2in), and preferably flat.

3. Then, use the steel tool to strike the flint downwards at a roughly 30-degree angle to create a spark that will catch on the awaiting char cloth or other tinder.

4. When the spark catches, blow gently on the char cloth/tinder. The ember will become brighter the more you blow. Be careful not to blow the flame out in your eagerness. It helps to do this in a windy area as it will encourage the char to take on the flame.

5. Keep blowing, as oxygen is critical at this point to encourage the tinder to catch. Soon, puff, puff, poof, you'll see the flames emerge from your tinder bundle!

6. Swiftly place it among your kindling and keep blowing until you see the fire taking hold.

◇◇◇◇◇◇◇◇◇◇◇◇◇◇◇◇◇◇◇

You can now add 'twisted fire starter' to your list of accolades! Let's hope you'll never need it in a serious survival situation but, if nothing else, it's a vital skill to have and to teach kids – and a pretty fun party trick.

A whole fire-starting flint and steel kit can be purchased from the online shop on my website *(see page 237)*.

CHAPTER 4

The Hill

As a child, I would find ways to escape the turbulent world and head to my place of sanctuary, which was a large hill at the back of my house, beyond several arable fields, which had lovely views from the top. One day, aged eight I believe, I took my dog, sneaked out and with a heavy heart climbed that hill. When I reached the top, I sat for a while before speaking out loudly to the universe. I wasn't sure who I was speaking to as I knew nothing about any teachings of Mother Earth or God, but I connected with something from such an early age that made me a very different child from my siblings and stand out in my environment.

I spoke out in my timid but determined voice: 'If you are listening, whoever you are, when I grow up, I want to change this world. I want there to be no more fighting, no more pain. Just peace.' I declared this in my childlike innocence believing anything was possible, as children do before they become lost and must 'grow up'. Pivotal moments in our childhood memory stay with us for a reason. The dreamworld wants us to remember them, so sends reminders when you come of age to deal with what lies ahead.

I feel my role now is to be a custodian of the land, an advocate for Mother Earth, like my ancestors before me. I need to be an example and a light to those who wish to see and to a generation of children who will know nothing of her great gifts and beauty. Their minds are locked up in a void of computers and social media where the main aim is to be popular for your own sake, not to benefit others or to care for our Earth. I have a sense that my life has been leading to this point – all paths, journeys, trials, battles, joys, suffering and success will be used. Nothing is wasted.

So often now we are told to 'find ourselves', 'discover our paths', 'find the real me'. Well, I honestly never needed to do that. I know exactly who I am, what I am, what I love, live and breathe for. My true self was there when I was born, and has been with me through every day of the years I have walked this Earth. Just as your true self has been with you since birth, finding moments between the good and bad times to reveal themselves to you. However, this presence in me did not mean I had always been free or able to thrive and be seen. We wear masks to prevent ourselves from revealing our truth to the world, to appease others, but these masks keep us awake at night or addicted to alcohol, drugs and various other vices.

Blood surges through my veins filled with a memory of a time that has long since passed, that has been all but eradicated.

I have no interest in what you do for a living, how much money you earn, what clothes or label you're wearing, how many friends or followers you have or how big your house or car is. The things you own are just that... objects you cannot take into the next world. Material possessions that might make you happy for a day... but just a day.

But I do want to know what you ache for, what you agonize over, what are you trying to remember, that which is engraved in your DNA. You have visions in your sleep, dreams in the day as you pass hundreds of fellow human beings without so much as a glance. We live in brick boxes detached from our true home, disconnected from each other, our communities, our food, the provision of life that Mother Earth has provided around us in abundance, disconnected from our water sources, our medicines or true feminine authority. We have forgotten who we are and how we were created. We are killing ourselves more and more as each day passes, by destroying the body that gives us life, the moon who gives us blood and creation who is the spirit of the world.

It's a Wednesday evening, 1 May 2019, three days before the new moon and 32 years after I climbed that hill in my youth. I sit by a different hill now, just 13km (8 miles) from the original. Unsure of what prompted me, other than an unwillingness to settle for life as it was then, I called out to the universe again and declared my life mission to heal her and restore great balance and peace. I asked her to show me the way and how I could achieve my aims. I took off my shoes and connected with her while I spoke and walked through the deep, wet grass. I felt the energy and felt grounded. There I let it go – into her arms.

Do you feel called to join me in this practice? Do you feel a tingle in your gut, a whisper in your left ear telling you this is your time, a niggle that said your name when I mentioned joining me? Well, don't ignore it, or allow your ego to confuse your thinking or tell you that your intuition doesn't work like mine or others does. Stepping out in fear is the only way to find what you're made of and why you're here. I have learned and now live by the rule – BE AFRAID AND DO IT

ANYWAY! That's where the power lies. So, when you can, wait for sunset, and step out onto the grass, or earth, and take off your shoes. Face the sun as she lowers in the sky. As you speak your heart to her, she will take your intention into the dark and plant the seed – when she rises in the morning it is done, planted. Then, let the magic begin; lift your arms to the sun, open your rib cage and stretch those muscles that hold the heart in place and protected. It's this that makes you exposed, vulnerable and open to her light. Your inhibitions will tell you that you look a fool, or that someone's watching, or that this is crazy. Just for once in your life tell those negative voices to be gone and take back your power. You are here for such an important reason, and she is calling you out of your monotony to fulfil the task set by your ancestors before they left this Earth. So, they're relying on you – the children and grandchildren of your line who are yet to come are relying on you and if you're reading this, the universe, or waterverse, wants you to know that YOU are the one you've been waiting for.

Take three deep breaths, pour out the words that come freely; tell the universe what you're longing for; ask her how you can find your purpose and then ask her to use you. Tell her what you're grateful for, the things you find most beautiful in the world, and tell her what hurts your heart. As you finish speaking your words, take three more breaths and, with me, exhale all you have spoken to the wind so that she may carry your story to the sun. Finally, as you exhale on the last breath, declare to the universe, waterverse and beyond, 'So be it. It is done.' Feel the weight of your body drop to the ground and lie back in the arms of Mother Earth and let her comfort you awhile, as the sun disappears over the horizon.

And never forget, as the universe proclaims: 'You are magically and wonderfully made. It is time to walk a new path. I've got you.'

Most of us go through life believing we are either lucky or unlucky in life, love, livelihood, circumstance, wealth or opportunity. From this day forwards, don't ever think in these terms. Luck is just a word that we use to explain away our misfortune or pain.

We are the orchestrators of our own destiny. As soon as you understand this your whole life will change. Truly. I tell you: The universe offers her hand daily to you and in our stubborn ignorance we reject her, believing that we deserve this, that we are lost, that we are not good enough. Our value in the world and our desires are not seen because we are poor or invisible, but because we are undervalued by the one person who we should be in love with – ourselves.

Every day you attract what you think. The mind is the most powerful force in this universe. If you believe your life will be shit, it will be. If you believe you will one day own a hundred beautiful sheep or inspire a few hearts, you will.

Life ticks by very fast. We miss so many opportunities believing that we are not good enough or that it is not the right time. Then we awake and feel this burning sensation in our bellies and realize that we have little time left to accomplish our dreams. Start today and don't ever give up. Don't listen to those voices of doubt when you weep in your bed alone at night; instead listen to the voices that encourage and show you the beauty inside your mind. For in the morning, you shall awake to re-write your story.

There is a wilderness in our modern lives that the Indigenous cultures of the world understand. These tribes – those still protecting, nurturing and living off the land – have the medicine, the wisdom, the spirit, the knowledge, the vision…. Let's go back, let's beg for forgiveness and redemption from the world we're destroying. Let's listen to the Earth, that gives everything life, once more. I believe so strongly that there is still time.

But the one thing I feel is lacking in my life, both personally and collectively, is a grandmother, a life-giving elder; a tribe of grandmothers, crones, wise medicine teachers who can guide us in the web of life. I crave that so much for, without her, every day I survive alone.

CHAPTER 5

Wolf

I have a soul kinship with wolves. I believe that we still have so much to learn from them and their social behaviour. I believe that they represent the very best of this world.

The Last Wolf

As I trek into the wilderness of life and wild nature, the wolf keeps knocking at the door of my heart. As a young lass growing up in a male-dominated society, in a family of strong Irish and Yorkshire men, ideas of living on the land and loving wolves were laughed at and shamed. When we look into the close connection between women and wolves, we can see how they mirror our sacred wild natures. We are both persecuted and misunderstood for this power.

Wolves and I have history long before I physically encountered them. I first met wolves at a sanctuary in the UK, then became adopted into the Wolf Clan of an Indigenous nation on Turtle Island before becoming the mother of a wolf hybrid cub, Aeyla, who I raised in my home.

The last alpha-female wolf in England allegedly was hunted and brutally killed at Humphrey Head, Cumbria, in 1390. Humphrey Head is a limestone outcrop situated between the villages of Allithwaite and Flookburgh. Here, it is claimed, the wolf was killed after a long and brutal pursuit by the son of a notorious wolf-hater, Sir Edgar Harrington. There is much debate about the exact moment of extinction of wolves from these isles – another tale claims the last wolf was killed in the 15th century on the site of Wormhill Hall, Derbyshire.

It matters not when wolves became extinct in England, but the point remains that wolves wander this landscape no more. I feel that the decline of this majestic animal marks the death of our wildness, on these shores and beyond.

The remains of wolves from prehistoric times that were found in caves suggest they were domesticated for protection and as hunting animals during the hunter-gatherer era. But I suspect our partnership with wolves was much deeper than that; it was a reciprocal relationship that benefitted both sides equally. We are now as far removed from our respect for wolves as we are from ourselves. The further we advance from our primal origins, our true wild and human nature, the more we seem to despise the very animal that reminds us of that original design and way of living. We see our reflection in their eyes and we fear what we have lost. We have lost our way and our ability to understand what it is to be wild, and what we do not understand we fear. What we fear we must eradicate, so that it can never remind us of our failings. With each wolf we kill, a little more of our true humanity dies with them. Although there are dark forces in this world, there is good at work, too, showing us in great detail the intricate nature of wolves and their close social and family bonds. Despite our relationship with our beloved pet dogs, their ancestors, the wolves, were not tolerated for long when the dawn of agriculture and farming arose in Britain. With the domestication of livestock, we began to see wolves as a threat to our food source.

> *'On the ragged edge of the world I'll roam. And the home of the wolf will be my home.'*
> **Robert W. Service**

The Wolf Family

Wolves form strong family and social groups, and they have deep emotions relating to all members of the pack. When one dies, they all visibly grieve for weeks. They feel the loss as deeply as would a human. This is not speculation; this was witnessed through extensive observations of the social life of wolves, which brought to light behaviours that had almost certainly never been witnessed before. Documented by Jim and Jamie Dutcher, who studied a pack of wolves in the Sawtooth Mountains, near central Idaho.

A story from Denali National Park in Alaska vividly shows the strong emotions binding wolf families together. In a small pack of wolves, a new alpha male and female had bonded and become partners and went on to mate, but their first litter of pups was taken by bears. They endured this loss together and went on to have another litter. One day they rallied – an excited howling and intense physical interaction and rubbing of each other in play – and went out west on a hunt. This pack lived safely within the national park, where wolves are protected legally, but trappers, intent on the destruction of the wolf, lie in wait on the invisible borders with traps for that fatal moment they cross. On this trip, when the pack stepped out of the safety of the park, the alpha female was captured in a barbaric leg trap. The alpha male and pups stayed by her side for days, but then the alpha male took the wolves back to the safety of the den. He returned every day to take food to his mate, but it was to no avail; her leg was injured in the metal trap that was tightening with each day and she was dying, in agony. After *two long weeks*, the trapper came out and found her. The alpha male ran for the woods and the trapper shot her in sight of her mate. When the alpha male returned, she was gone and he stood and howled for her every night for weeks. Wolves know love and despair and yet we treat them like savages. They (men) try to eradicate wolves like they try to eradicate women.

In history, we used to live alongside wolves and they would help us hunt. But men began to see them as a threat, in much the same way as they saw women as a threat when they displayed great spiritual powers connected to nature and medicine, and persecuted them as witches. If the wolves die out, I fear that is woman's fate, too. We must protect the wolf in order to save ourselves.

The seeds of our future take root in the chaos of childhood and emerge in the mature valley of midlife and motherhood. They lie in wait for the right time and push forth their delicate green fronds of life along the road less travelled. This seed of mine has a warped sense of humour and made a wild child – a wolf guardian with a fierce heart and a shepherdess of sheep. I guess I was put here to break all the rules and define the term 'wolf in sheep's clothing'!

But mostly, I was made to be a guardian of the wolf and embody the return of the symbiotic sacred relationship between wolves and prey, and to challenge the notion that wolves are a threat to our species and food. Those with the power to make decisions, who approve the culling of wolves from the wild, do not realize that the destruction of their intimate family groups exacerbates the problem of livestock attacks on their farms and ranches. Why? Because when a pack is allowed to form naturally, without intervention or fear of constant attack, they form exceptionally tight bonds, with each member playing a vital role in the hierarchy of structure, function and family, especially when it comes to making a kill and feeding their pups. In this system, a pack will take its prime source of food from the wild, from elk, moose, bison or deer, rather than from livestock. This behaviour has been proven over years of extensive research.

The issues arise when hunters move in and kill the alphas or mid-ranking adults, who naturally put themselves in harm's way to protect the other wolves – a sacrifice with catastrophic repercussions. When an elder or alpha is killed, it's like the remaining pack have lost their mother or father. Without a defined authority figure to make decisions and be responsible for it, the pack loses the knowledge and experience that tells the wolves where to roam and how to hunt, including the ability to take down big wild animals. As a result, the pack no longer avoids livestock and the wrath of some (not all) ranchers, who are intent on destroying every last one of these vital, most-needed beings.

Sometimes, the pack will break apart – its members dispersing far and wide. The last thing a lone wolf wants is to be a lone wolf; they need family, community. Out in the wild alone, they need to catch the easiest prey possible, expending minimal energy, and at times this will happen to be livestock.

So, you see, we create the problem and, in our rage to protect 'our world', we see the only option as the eradication of the entire species, without realising the cycle of nature and how ecosystems and environments work. We need these keystone species to stop the overpopulation of prey that can decimate our delicate forests and habitats.

Recently, a devastating case of wolf torture emerged, committed in the name of 'management'. A man called Cody Roberts of Daniel, Wyoming, ran down a pack of wolves on a snow machine, captured a young, 9-month-old female wolf pup and tortured her, parading her around his local bar with her mouth taped shut, letting his dogs attack her and shocking her with an electric collar. Once he'd seen her in enough pain, mocking her all the while, he took her out the back and shot her. This behaviour came to light because he was stupid enough to film it. However, this is *not* an isolated incident. Terrifyingly, this act is *legal* in Wyoming and many other US states.

This case affected me deeply and I will commit the rest of my days to being a guardian of the wolves so that barbaric events like what happened to Hope, as this precious wolf was called, *never* happen again.

Why on this good earth are we allowing our precious creatures to be trapped, tortured and killed in this way? This case shook the world and many organizations are calling for lasting change and for wolves to be relisted on the protection list. We must do better; we must protect these wild beings.

The number of livestock killed by wolves worldwide each year is so small that it's insignificant compared to how many animals die due to poor human management, disease and other predators. So, why do people blame wolves? I believe that they have become scapegoats for the hatred men feel towards their own kind, their miserable lives, their inability to control what cannot be controlled. Wolves embody freedom. Ironically, wolves hold all the values these so-called hunters admire and apparently pride themselves and their 'constitutions' on: strength, honour, tenacity and the will to fight to the death to protect their family.

Wolves can even suffer heartbreak. Take the story of Cinderella, a wolf from the Druid Peak pack in Yellowstone National Park, USA. Cinderella earned her name after enduring years of attacks from her sister before finally standing up to her, helped by other pack members, and eradicating her sister's authority over the pack. Cinderella was transformed from a submissive to a dominant female, and went on to lead with a gentle, strong nature until she died in 2004. After her death, her alpha male who had birthed many pups with her, went to the top of a nearby hill, curled up in a ball and died. And they say wolves are ruthless, heartless killers. I say that wolves are some of the most intelligent, loving, playful, important creatures and true stories like this demonstrate that without question.

First Encounter

Anyone who truly understands me knows my connection to, and love of, the wolf. It's been there since I was a child, and throughout my life I have grown closer to the wild wolf within. The wolf came to me in dreams as I was growing up. It is the night walker that shapeshifts into our consciousness when we are uneducated, naive and largely unaffected by a world that doesn't believe in magic. I dreamed that a black wolf came to me and then a storm rolled in; the clouds and lightning were multicoloured. The modern rational world says the wolf is coming to harm me and will cause turbulence, so be afraid. Fear, fear and more fear. But what if the wolf saw and felt the storm coming before I did, and the multicoloured clouds were there because the power of the storm was charging up all the chakras? Maybe the wolf was standing beside me to guard me through the storm of light and colour, preparing me for the forthcoming transformation. Perspective is everything and as a child I had no fear of the wolf. Only the world wanted me to be afraid. Little Red Riding Hood tried to fool me, the Three Little Pigs tried to fool me, but I have a deep affinity with the underdog – the one who is unfairly bullied and mocked. I champion them, and so I followed the wolf. Something in me as a child recognized something in them.

As an adult, my first encounter with wolves was at a hidden location in England, where I volunteered. At first, I watched and studied their behaviour on short trips when my son Harry was with his dad. Then, Harry started to come with me, and we stayed in a little shack on the hillside right above the forest that was home to seven wolves. This was a sanctuary that rescued lone wolves from illegal breeders or who had been rejected from packs and almost killed, because owners, such as zoos, simply didn't understand the social structure of a wolf pack – you cannot just throw a group of unrelated wolves together and expect them to get along. Even family wolf packs were not equipped for confinement. In the wild, some youngsters leave to set up their own packs, or head out as lone wolves to join existing packs many miles away from where they were born. This is impossible in captivity, so there would be serious infighting and the rejects who couldn't leave would often be attacked by rival wolves.

The wolf came to me in dreams as I was growing up. It is the night walker that shapeshifts into our consciousness when we are uneducated, naive and largely unaffected by a world that doesn't believe in magic.

The first full-blood wolf I ever met was an 11-year-old grey timber wolf from North America. It is said that wolves can hear your heart beating and react according to if they feel a threat or love. Her ears must have been ringing from the drumming thuds coming from my chest full of love. I felt my heart racing in excitement and awe, and I knew she could sense it. I knelt and she approached me. We caught each other's eye and I swear we both mutually bowed to each other. My heart exploded to be acknowledged by a creature so wild, fierce and spirited! That memory is forever carved into my bones and tears fell down my face as I saw the sadness in her eyes. She couldn't disguise it with the big shimmering silver mane around her face. She was sad not just because of her enclosure, but because her species was one of the most hated in the world. And I felt that, deeply. Then quietly, in my soul, I reiterated my commitment to be a guardian of the wolf from that day forwards. That night, on the eve of my 40th birthday, Harry and I were settling down for the night by the wood stove in the cabin. We slept on the wooden floor in our sleeping bags. Harry had just drifted off, it was 11:45 p.m., and one of the wolves started to sing, then another, until they all joined together in the most enchanting cacophony of shrills and howls, chatter and deep belly grunts that could be heard several miles away across the valley. *They're wishing me Happy Birthday*, I thought, as I stared into the inky night, beaming from ear to ear.

This life is a balance between the things we dream of, long for, hope for and nurture. It's not about the things we are successful at or achieve. It's the journey that matters – the choices we make and the paths we follow, of which nothing is wasted.

As I awoke on my birthday, I was aware of the reality of where I was on this journey of life and how the things I'd manifested and dreamed about countless times in my life had led me to be there, in that spot. I had spent the night listening to tawny owls hooting at each other in their mating rituals and now I sat with my strong brew of Yorkshire tea, on a bench with a view across a deep valley welcoming me into the next season of my life. With the warmth of the sun on my face and the sky crystal blue, I watched the trees in myriad greens coming forth from spring growth into maturity. Swallows chirped and soared overhead, as did the buzzard who glided through the thermals above the pine forest opposite. There was a rushing stream in the distance with an echo that far exceeded its actual size. As I sat silently looking at the valley below, accompanied by the orchestral rhymes of dawn birdsong, I saw flashes through the trees. By the time I got my binoculars, they'd gone. I waited patiently and before long, again, more flashes. This time out came the wolf, the glorious light shining on her fur in a blaze of browns and grey. What a privilege, to be honoured by the presence of an animal so persecuted by humans. Their presence is so strong, it's humbling beyond words.

In human company, I struggle; I am awkward and fight thoughts of doubt and inferiority. But with wolves and all that's natural, I am completely at one, with no fear or worry, just a longing to protect what we so often destroy.

Not long after my meeting with Kai, the timber wolf, another rescue arrived called Bear. He only lived for six months. We saw him step out of his cage into the wide world and the joy he had in those six months was worth every ounce of grief that came afterwards. This wolf was so small in stature, so lost and misplaced from the very beginning. He left this world surrounded by love and hope, with humans by his side, cradling his head as he took his last breath. It was a world away from his troublesome beginnings, persecuted and caged. From the start, he was bound, neglected, isolated and alone, deprived of the natural world and never to experience true socialization within a family pack, such as battles with siblings for a higher place in the pecking order. He never saw the water, blue sky or grass that his spirit and soul craved. All he knew was life in the hands of those who wished to harm and destroy his species, one of the most important ecologically and spiritually ever to have walked our planet. From birth, his destiny was planned.

Some people, some animals, some spirits are not destined for this world. They were not made to be caged; their wings are too bright. Bear was too bright, too clever, too cunning, too fast and too tortured to stay long. He was gone too soon, like the loss of sunlight with the rising of the moon. Now he is running with the wolves in the star camps. He is finally free; free to run with the wind, where he belongs.

Some men say we shouldn't anthropomorphize animals, shouldn't give them feelings or emotions. Maybe that is because men still live in a world where their fellow women have been killed as witches for believing and understanding the behaviour of animals. Explain to me why the timber wolf Kai died three days after Bear died. Kai had been alone for many years and as soon as Bear arrived, she took him under her wing. They were often seen chasing each other around their enclosure. They ate together, Kai often sharing her food with the growing pup. They slept in the same den together. They became inseparable. In my opinion, when Bear did not return from the vet (he died from flystrike), Kai just knew his spirit had gone. I sense she felt his spirit leave the Earth. Animals can die of broken hearts, as humans can. I have experienced it many times in the animals I've cared for and I'm sure you could tell me of an occasion where this has happened to your beloved pet or animal, too.

We have removed ourselves from their world, the world in which we, too, belong. I'd like to go there, to that world that is real and natural. Animals live in the now, where there's no judgement, no aspiration for success, no shame and none of the turmoil experienced in the human realm – only survival, purpose, connection, love, sex and death.

Women and Wolves

Women and wolves share the same soul. The witches knew it; the plants and moon know it. The alpha lurks and prowls, waiting to emerge in you. She waits for a sign, a symbol, like a forgotten language lost in time that only the woman and wolf can summon and then recognize. It takes another woman, or wolf, to call you out into the wild, away from the cage and guide you to safety. That's my role, my purpose: to bring women back to their powerful, feral, wild selves, so that they may continue to raise wolf cubs. The wild woman and wolf will not be tamed; she cannot be domesticated. She threatens the male-dominated world because her instincts warn her to resist that which destroys nature. Now do we walk alongside her or away from her? Many have to deny the call of the wild woman and wolf inside to survive. A lone wolf and woman pose little threat, but together, when working as a pack, they are a force to be reckoned with. Women should unite. We must rebel against the way we've been conditioned to react to other women as a threat. Men rarely compete like this and although they stand on fellow men to get to the top, they also give each other a hand up because there's plenty of room for them up there!

This idea is not to threaten men. Please don't confuse our rising strength with the fall of man. It is wholeheartedly to redress the balance in our world. The law of the universe shows us that all things should be equal; the positive ion does not function without the negative. After thousands of years of oppression, the woman and the wolf do not hold on to bitterness, we are just desperate for a world where we can live without our survival and adrenal systems working in overdrive and fearing for our children's lives.

Woman and wolf, our shadows are aligned – the wolf's spirit matches ours with fierce tenderness. We shall stalk the forest kingdoms of the Earth and the mountain ranges of the mind in pursuit of peace, protection and the restoration of our precious wild home.

The Two Wolves Within

There's a battle in my mind between two wolves – we all have them. The battle of wills is very real for me. In my encounters with male authority there was one wolf, Demelza (yes, both of my inner wolves have names), who wanted to people please, be accepted and not put up a fight against injustice or mistreatment. I would not have accepted physical abuse, but I wanted peace with all my heart. So, I gave in to the overwhelming pressure to accept the woman I was then, to know my place and not have an opinion on anything that might disrupt the peace of behaving in the way this world teaches us to behave. I also felt that being attractive was the way to get noticed and recognized in this world.

And then there is Brida, the wolf who won't let me sleep…. The wolf that keeps pawing at me as I close my eyes, to go hunting with her in the realm of day dreams. She is fierce and unforgiving, and knows the path we must walk daily. But I battle against her. Sometimes

I'm afraid of what she will reveal, of what she will ask of me. But I respect her the most of both the wolves. She is the boldness that stands beside me through all my trials. She is truth and tenderness with unshakeable strength.

What are the names of your wolves? Do you see them in your trip around Asda? Who chooses what? Do you see them scrolling through your phone? Which accounts do they follow? Our ability to fully comprehend the power of our minds, and the power of our behavioural traits is vital, as the path we take is determined by the choices we make based on which wolf we feed with attention.

Try naming your wolves. Decide which wolf, based on their name, is in charge of your thoughts and actions. Are you in control of this wolf or does she control you? If things are consistently going wrong for you, or you feel lost or unsure of your purpose here, maybe you're feeding the wrong wolf. Speak with them, tell the dominant wolf to step down, thank them for their protection, but say that you do not need them to keep doing that. However, you would like them to stay and keep a balance between good and bad, dark and light, positive and negative. Then, bring forth the wolf who lingers in the shadows, beckon her to come and feed with you and then ask her to walk with you awhile. Ask her to show you a new path where all of the truth that hides in the darkness will come to light. Treat this communion as a sacred interaction between you and the wolfkin. Lay out food for her, give thanks under the light of the moon and ask her to walk with you daily. For when testing times come, and they will, you will sense the guardian wolf brush past your cheek with her tail to remind you that she is in there watching, circling the fire at night in your dreams, hoping you will come to feed her and her pure heart, so that you might gain wisdom from the visions you see when in her presence.

Wolf Moon

Why are wolves seen howling at the moon? Is it because the moon is as much their grandmother as she is ours? The main difference in our relationship is that wolves know how to honour the moon and utilize her power – something we have forgotten. When the moon is in her full or new cycle, your intuition is sharp and your senses heightened. This is when the wolf within wakes in you to release you from your slumber of conditioning. The wolf moon offers enlightenment. It is time to climb into the craters of the moon in your mind, where you have hidden what you fear facing. It's time to come home. The wolf is waiting to show you the way, to guide you and guard you through your life and, most of all, show you the truth of your existence here on this planet.

Be ready when you do this, though. If you speak with conviction, it means everything of insignificance falls away around you. Traits and behaviours that no longer serve your spirit and purpose are culled from consciousness. People, relationships, blockages and shame are filtered away. All that remains is the echo of a life lived and a new life yet to come. Ask the wolf moon to use you. Howl that longing of a life you want to live into existence.

When I struggle in earthly terms, I call on the wolf. She guides me to the root, to my bloodline, the forest of solitude and safety. Here, I will lick my wounds and dwell in the protection of her spirit and stand strong in the assurance that the sun will always rise again tomorrow.

Wolf Cub

I always wondered if I'd be blessed with raising a wolf like they have raised me. A year before writing this book, I was staring at the full storm moon on the 17th day of March, not realising that she'd deliver me this little gift under her light. A year later, I'm staring at the full storm moon and there are wolf eyes looking back at me.

I raised Aeyla, a Gray wolf hybrid cub, from the day she was born, in my tiny house. As I glance across at her now, the size of a small elephant, her silver and black winter coat glistening in the moonlight, I wonder HOW? Then I remember what brought me to this place. I asked for it, for her, and she came, with claws, teeth, limbs like a giraffe and a spirit as free as the wind. She must take after me, we are one.

It was my choice to raise Aeyla from birth after her mum couldn't. It had been a difficult birth and her mother had rejected her. I didn't need to think twice and drove to collect her from Scotland on a 14-hour round trip. Since then, I've been learning what it's like to be a mama to a wildling and, believe me, it's a rollercoaster and not a role taken on lightly. But I have the intuition and experience needed and this is, I believe, destiny in all its magic and wonder. I spent the first 12 weeks keeping her alive, feeding her every two hours through the night, and have raised her to be a confident, courageous, happy young wolf-hybrid pup. This is no mean feat as you have to understand their physiology, spirit, anatomy and character in order to succeed. No one should take on the extremely challenging task of raising a cub without understanding the serious, unwavering commitment required and without a deep desire to understand their behaviour. Even for me, with plenty of experience, this was nothing like raising a labrador or a terrier. Wolf dogs are by their very nature incredibly advanced, demanding and vocal, and require a firm stance if they are going to live in your home and with your family. This task was brought to me, I believe, to demonstrate the wolf dog's character and its ability to be well trained around livestock and people.

I wonder how many shepherds in the history of shepherding have not only had a wolf dog as a companion, but also taken them with them while lambing? Well, Aeyla does all of that and takes it in her stride.

Aeyla and I... the misfit wolves among sheep. The sacred feminine bubbling inside me will always be indebted to the wolf for her tenacity and reliance. She dwells within me and is my passion, fierce resolve and wisdom. She lives forever not only as an engraving tattooed on my arm, but in a chamber of my heart.

CHAPTER 6

Dreams

D reams are the manifestation of things that, for a time, we can only visualize in our imagination and are brought to us through our subconscious.

They are wishes for a place where you are the best, most authentic version of yourself, in another landscape, livelihood, love and life.

They are wishes for a better world – a place where there are no tears or heartache for you, your family, nations, our animal kingdom, trees or our Mother Earth.

They are hopes for peaceful relationships.

They are childhood visions and fairy tales you once believed.

They are magic and wonder.

They are the impossible – those paths that seem unachievable.

They are deep desires and bountiful expectations.

Dreams are achievable if you never stop learning, and NEVER underestimate yourself, even if others do.

Dreams are an ocean away – light years away.

They are the thoughts you have when you are woken in the early morning by the light of the moon.

But I tell you... dreams do come true.

If you speak them every day. If you truly believe in them and you set intentions, plans and paths in your head. Visualize it. Taste it. Become it. Catch it.

You must always have a dream... and whatever you do, NEVER let it go.

I think dreaming is a huge part of why we are lacking connection in this world. When we wake after a night of terror or meaningful dreams, we don't deal with them, or acknowledge them, we just move on with our day. So, the dreams stagnate or get lost. Then, we wonder why we feel like shit the next day, perhaps for a few days. How many dreams have you had where you wished you could have translated their meaning? We need more interpreters and dream-weavers in the world. Dreams need to be discussed, not just as something we wish to achieve in life, but as a deep subconscious tap on the shoulder that is trying to show you the way.

The alchemy of dreams and the mysteries of the inner self – these are the universe's way of illuminating what and who we are; a road into our souls.

During some phases in the moon's cycle, my dreams are so intense that they wreck my days with tiredness while I'm processing their meaning. Since childhood, I've lived by them and they've shaped so many of my decisions. But we may feel embarrassed to speak about them or allow them to take residence in our minds for too long, because they often bring challenges. I believe that speaking out about your dreams and wishes will not only do something positive deep within your psyche that will manifest them, but vocalizing them also allows them to be heard in the spirit world. You must believe you are heard; you are connected to those dreams; you are the reason they were sent. You are not pulled towards certain things without a reason. It's part of your journey and you either go after it… or let it go.

CHAPTER 7

The Wisdom of Sheep

Sheep play an important role in our history and our survival as a species. Once, they were sacred animals and they have long been utilized for the multitude of resources they offer us from their bodies, including meat, hides, wool, bones and tallow. Sheep were one of the first animals to be domesticated and they are now treated with such little respect, which is a reflection of how we have lost touch with our very nature and capacity to survive. In a world of convenience, materialism and corporate greed, the humble sheep is seen just as a commodity.

I plan to change that. My ancestors had a plan for me that involved an animal I'd never so much as glanced at before. I never grew up wanting to be a shepherd, but shepherding, and being a custodian of the land, found me and put me on the path of the old ways, of the ancient ones. Starting a wool business led me to shepherd more than just sheep. I now have a successful wool business that sends my products all over the world. I don't own a farm, but I long for one. I live in a council house and rent land where I can for my flock. I am not from a farming family, but my ancestors ran woollen mills in

Foxford, County Mayo, Ireland, and I fell in love with these creatures later in my life. I'm sure I am born of a different breed. I may be a shepherd, but I have visions much bigger than a field of sheep!

Sheep are like people. Some can follow and have a relatively easy yet mundane life of order and formation, while others are more wild and natural leaders, who find adventure in escape, greener pastures, and have the strength not to follow the crowd – much to the shepherd's dismay! How do we leave the flock behind in search of pastures new? How do we break out of the nine-to-five routine and build a homestead, grow and raise our own organic food, and use plant medicine to holistically manage and honour our animals in all we do and make from them? I'll shepherd you.

First, I shall explain why sheep deserve every ounce of respect we can muster. From the plains of ancient Mesopotamia to the Viking warriors of Scandinavia and rolling English countryside, sheep have been central to the story of humanity and our evolution. Our ancestors began domesticating sheep thousands of years ago; since then, they have helped us win wars, clothed our bodies, furnished our homes, fed us and the trade in their products has financed nations. Splendid monasteries and churches are standing in all their architectural glory today because of sheep. Industries were built on the back of their wool, merchants and shepherds thrived, and meat trading changed the landscape of our towns and cities. However, the rich, grand and exuberant tapestry sheep wove into our past is sadly forgotten by many today.

Over 8 million years ago, the oldest known ancestor of modern sheep evolved in the cold mountains of Central Asia. During the last Ice Age, these high-altitude creatures, the Asiatic mouflon – a dark-coloured, hairy animal with a soft, woolly undercoat – began to move. Some ambled west, some east and on into Siberia, some even made it as far as North America, crossing the frozen Bering Strait around 750,000 years ago. The breed contributed to creating the modern domesticated sheep we see today. These bovines had large horns and naturally shed their fleece each year. Then, around 11,000 years ago, hunter-gatherer cultures turned their attention to growing and farming in an area that has become known as the Fertile Crescent, which stretches across the Middle East from Egypt through to the Persian Gulf. People in this region began growing crops and they began to domesticate animals, including sheep.

With the domestication of sheep came the need for someone to look after these unruly, walking woolly jumpers and protect them from thieves, wolves, bears and other predators, as well as leading them to fresh forage. It is clear from archaeological finds that shepherding is an ancient profession. There is evidence that a more settled way of life was already taking hold when the huge stones and megaliths of ancient Britain, such as the Avebury stones in Wiltshire and the stones of Callanish on the Isle of Lewis, were being erected about 5,000 years ago.

Sheep are grass-munching, nature-friendly mowers and provide the best fertilizer you can find. Sheep love a good bite of fresh grass and can graze for eight to 10 hours at a time. The grass is barely chewed before swallowing – when the magic happens. After the swallowed grass has been in their stomachs for about an hour, sheep regurgitate it back into their mouths and begin chewing. One of my favourite things is to watch my flock as the ball of grass re-emerges up their necks into their mouths. They chew for 10 seconds then swallow again. This process is called chewing the cud. They repeat this until it's time for the grass to move down into the second of their four stomachs. Their efficiency in grazing well means large swathes of land are needed, not only for fresh food but to fulfil all the requirements of their diet. Sheep are generally easy to look after, but only if you give them what they need. However, problems arise quite rapidly when you don't maintain their health or habitat.

I manage my flock organically and as naturally as possible on the limited rental land I can access. I use the method of managed migration, which mimics the grazing and browsing behaviour of the animals if they were free to roam. If I had hundreds of acres, managed migration could be implemented much more effectively, for the benefit of the land and animals. Sheep are herd animals, so they move slowly through an area and selectively graze out invasive grasses, creating space for dormant and delicate wildflowers to emerge, while also trampling in any seeds for germination, locking in carbon as they compact the ground and fertilising the soil with their dung. These benefits are why environmentalists use this method, as well as agroforestry and silvopastoral management (where trees are grown between crops and animals graze the land after the growing season).

Grazing helps local insect populations thrive because it leaves some flowers for pollination and encourages regrowth. Parasite burdens are minimized by not leaving sheep on the same ground for too long and, therefore, I never need to worm my sheep. If a sheep displays scouring (diarrhoea) many think that it needs worming, but usually it is due to a lack of minerals in their diet because the soils are so depleted. Minerals like cobalt, selenium, magnesium, iodine and copper are decimated in our grasslands, so they need to be replaced every year to avoid ailments in the flock, such as scouring, wool rot, bad feet, foot rot, scald, certain neurological conditions and parasite burdens. You can check your flock's faeces or do a blood test to check the minerals in your sheep and replace as necessary.

Minerals can be replaced in the form of a mineral bucket, liquid drench or a bolus. A bolus is a short bullet-shaped tablet, in this case containing the key minerals for optimal health in the flock, especially through winter. The bolus ingeniously sits in the gut and leeches the minerals gradually over a period of four to six months. If you do need to worm your sheep you can go for the standard chemical solutions or you can follow my more natural method and recipe, which is more time-consuming but kinder to their gut, the land, insects and your wallet.

A RECIPE FOR WORMING SHEEP

I grind up a mix of herbs and spices known to rid the digestive system of parasites in humans and livestock. These include:

◊ wormwood

◊ black walnut

◊ diatomaceous earth

◊ cumin

◊ cayenne

◊ garlic

◊ ginger

◊ rosemary

◊ thyme

Use the powdered form or grind up the seeds.

The powder is then filled into a small bolus-making machine and I administer them at a dose of two per sheep over a period of three days. If stored in an airtight container, the powder will keep for years.

◇◇◇◇◇◇◇◇◇◇◇◇◇◇◇◇◇◇

Other natural remedies include ivy leaves for a gut problem, and willow leaves and bark for a natural painkiller (they contain salicin, the same compound found in aspirin). Another tonic that works for mastitis in sheep is a mixture of oregano and garlic water. Sometimes, I make a cleansing balm for myself and the flock.

If you have any problems with lice or scab in your animals, try rubbing diatomaceous earth against the skin or use one of the many products you can buy from the local country store. If the grass shoots away in the spring growing season, it often won't have time to take up enough magnesium, so this must be supplemented.

Finally, you may have heard of flystrike, aka blowfly. If you're a farmer, you definitely have. This, as a shepherd, is the bane of my life. It has taken more sheep than anything else, because they are so hard to detect until it's too late. Medically termed myiasis, flystrike dermatitis is a skin condition characterized by the invasion of maggots under the skin of the animal. It can occur in all animals, but the flies are particularly attracted to an open wound or smelly, poo-ridden wool on a sheep. Within a matter of hours of the flies laying eggs, the maggots hatch and start burrowing into the skin of the sheep. If not caught soon enough, it can be fatal within a matter of hours.

Vigilance is needed to prevent flystrike. I have used some of the harsh chemicals on the market in the past, but I have found them to be very ineffective over the time period they claim to protect the sheep. As my flock is relatively small and I interact with them often, I make my own natural potion.

A METHOD FOR PREVENTING FLYSTRIKE

1. Find an old spray bottle – the kind you use to spray indoor plants, or any bottle with a good spray nozzle.

2. Fill half the bottle with neem oil and the remainder with several drops of eucalyptus essential oil, citrus oil, tea tree oil, apple cider vinegar and washing-up liquid (to emulsify the mixture). In cold temperatures, it will become solid so warm it up before use.

3. Spray it every week or two when interacting with your sheep, such as at feeding or fussing time.

◇◇◇◇◇◇◇◇◇◇◇◇◇◇◇◇◇◇◇

If you do encounter the dreaded flystrike, you will need to gently shear away the affected area and scrape away all maggots from the wounds. Then, apply an antibacterial wound spray and maggot-killing products bought from a country store. It is evident to me that the prevalence of flystrike may be hereditary, so sheep that are prone to it may need to be culled for the health of the flock. In my flock, it's likely that Bonnie has the hereditary gene as she gets flystrike most years no matter what I do – but she ain't going anywhere!

Managed migration definitely helps with flystrike. The sheep are moved regularly to imitate natural movement and I do this using electric-fencing systems between fenced paddocks. One of the only defence mechanisms sheep have is their ability to flock together, making it harder for predators to pick off a lone sick one. I have observed within my flock that even though sheep spend most of their time with their faces down, grazing, making them vulnerable to predators, there is always one or two sheep who stay alert and on guard. While the flock is chewing the cud, the leader sheep stand with their heads aloft and alert; they then give a little grunt if danger is approaching (in the form of a human or a dog).

The one job that all shepherds need to do, whether using managed migration or not, is to count their sheep, no matter how many are in the flock. We count to check for strays or any sick sheep, and make head counts at lambing time and when sorting them for shearing, market and sales. Yes, it is possible to do this without falling asleep, especially as animals have this annoying habit of moving! Have you ever tried counting moving objects quickly, many of them mingled together? Our ancestors developed a clever and very memorable way of counting their flocks. Originating within both branches of the Celtic language, the old Yan Tan Tethera system was used in most parts of Britain before the industrial revolution, but particularly in Scotland, the Lake District and the Yorkshire Dales. The system is vigesimal (based on the number 20) and after counting to 20, the shepherd would make a notch on their crook or move a pebble from one pocket to another, before continuing to another 20 and so on.

The Swaledale version of the counting system is:

1. Yan	11. Yanadick
2. Tan	12. Tanadick
3. Tether	13. Tetheradick
4. Mether	14. Metheradick
5. Pip	15. Bumfit
6. Azer	16. Yanabum
7. Sezer	17. Tanabum
8. Akker	18. Tetherabum
9. Conter	19. Metherabum
10. Dick	20. Jigget

So, what type of sheep to keep? Although I believe that individual pedigree sheep breeds should be protected and promoted for their heritage in our history of livestock breeding and domestication, I also believe you can have a spectacular and unique line of breeding with the cross of two or more separate breeds. This would be done to combine multiple successful traits. For example, my breed of 'Shetlandics' is a cross of the northern short-tail breeds, including the Shetland, Icelandic, Hebridean, Boreray and Manx. This wild cross-breed has great qualities. They are tame, sociable, affectionate and wise. They are great milking mothers who need minimal intervention at lambing and produce wool in various gorgeous shades that mimic the colours of the landscape. I named them 'Shetlandics' many years ago and I now see the name being recognized and used more widely. It is exciting to think of their recognition in a world full of white sheep!

My 'Shetlandics' have a ferocious will to survive. They are so extremely tough that they won't tell you they're unwell until they're on their death bed. Although it is clever not to show weakness with predators around, it is annoying for the shepherd who loves them and would quite like them to live. They carry many wild characteristics that increase their ability to survive well. They graze well on poor forage and are strong and hardy, even in the harshest weather, because the northern short-tail breeds like mine store fat around their internal organs to protect them in the cold climate. Commercial breeds do not do this and store fat around their back and rump, where the meat is abundant. My flock have descended from the Old Norse sheep that travelled across from Scandinavia during the time of the Vikings, after all. They were once known as seaweed-eating sheep, and are used to grazing on volcanic and mineral-rich soils that gives them all the minerals they need and gives their meat an exceptional flavour. They give birth outdoors in the elements, so their circadian rhythm is not disrupted.

They are a slow-growing meat breed that will usually be ready to go for meat from 18 to 24 months, after a happy life in as natural an environment as possible. Meat at this age is called hogget. At two to three years, it is known as mutton (which is making a comeback as it is full of flavour). Many lambs are sent to slaughter at the age of four months – this does not sit well with me and nor would it with the shepherds of old. In the rush to make quick money, we have forgotten the role sheep have played in our society for thousands of years.

I have worked as a contract shepherdess on some farms where sheep were treated as a possession to be commodified; now I work to try and change that perception and practice. In the few places where I found standards lower than acceptable, I tried to implement change. The main issue I found on these farms was a pressure to get jobs done quickly for various reasons. With speed comes stress and a high level of adrenaline, pressure and anxiety for a job to go smoothly and quickly. But we're talking about working with animals here and sheep, in particular, have an unpredictable nature. They may fool you into thinking they're going to walk through a corall (pen) calmly but then, at the last minute, they shoot you a sly glance, then spring like a gazelle on acid over the last hurdle, out to relative freedom before you can catch them.

Despite popular opinion, sheep are intelligent and wise. They know how to find medicine in the hedgerow, often guided by the leader sheep. They know when to stop eating the medicine before it becomes toxic. They can recognize people, cars and familiar landscapes.

Something I noticed in my flock when I sit pondering life with them, is that they change their behaviour the more you interact with them and build trust. We don't often spend time with our animals because of 'busyness' but I have a fascination with the behaviour of all animals and, as I interact with them every day, I get to witness their unique traits. Sheep are very much like elephants or wolves: there is a matriarch or leader sheep and a very defined pecking order within the flock. Bonnie is my oldest sheep. At the age of 11, she dictates the behaviour in the flock. She takes them to the tastiest hedgerows and decides when the flock will stop grazing and rest. She leads many successful and unsuccessful escape attempts in search of someone's allotment and prized cabbages (yes, it happened). She is also the first to lead the other yows (we call ewes 'yows' in Yorkshire) to see a new member of the flock once it's born. It brings me such joy to see grandmothers coming up to see their granddaughters and nuzzle them. There is a clear display of congratulation and happiness as a new lamb and a new mother are welcomed into the clan.

In the spring of 2023, I had just begun lambing in the Yorkshire Dales on a fellow shepherdess's farm. A group of my best yows came with me and I had started to lamb. Danu was such a calm, gentle little yow with a beautiful fleece of silvery grey locks. She was three years old and had been with me from birth. Like the other girls in my flock, she was precious, selected for all of her top-quality traits, and loved a cuddle. This was her first time lambing and I was so excited to have one of her lambs to continue her line of good nature and fleece quality. She gave birth to a cute little black lamb, full of life, and she instantly loved her, cleaning her and licking her all over, while nuzzling and making low chattering noises to encourage her lamb to stand and start feeding. I named her Betty. Danu was so proud of Betty that she paraded her around the field to show the other yows and to find the sweetest grass.

I saw all was well with Danu and Betty before continuing with my rounds and lambing around 1,000 yows. Claire, the farm owner, helped me to keep an eye on my flock while I was doing my rounds, which took about 14 hours each day. Soon after Danu gave birth, I walked down to my lambing field to see a glorious sunrise, and as the warmth heated the land, a mist rose from the valleys and forest and hung like dragon's breath across the dale. I was excited to see if any of my yows had lambed overnight. My excitement very quickly waned when I saw Danu dead at the gate. I still don't know how she died; it could have been one of many things. Little Betty stood over her still warm body, bleating for her to get up so that she could feed. I fought back the tears and grabbed Betty before she could bolt across the field.

What happened next not only grieved me, but also Claire, who had never seen such human-like behaviour from a domestic sheep before. We brought Betty into the warm barn and settled her into a pen of straw with a few other lambs that had been brought inside. Betty displayed such visible grief at the loss of her mother, it was incredibly hard to watch. She refused to eat, so I fed her using a tube, but that can only be done for a few days to avoid damaging a sheep's throat. We tried medicine and homeopathic belladonna and aconite for shock. Then she started to become unwell in her gut. She didn't understand why she had been taken from her mum and, though she came through several ailments, she only fed half-heartedly. Two weeks went past and she didn't play with the other lambs, who were bouncing around by now and feeding ferociously. Betty stood quietly in the corner and, day by day, gradually stopped taking food at all. She gave up; she didn't want to live. She could have recovered but her will had been taken when her mother died. Then, 20 days after Danu died, Betty did, too, for no apparent reason other than a broken heart. I was glad she did in the end. Seeing her visibly sad eyes was heart-breaking to myself and Claire, who put so much effort into saving her. As I did with Danu, I skinned her of her fleece and took out her heart to bury with her mother's down in the woods – together again. I have both of their sheepskins now as a reminder of their life with me. Short though it was, it was full of love and not wasted.

Lambing – the Portal

This time of year provides the bread and butter of my work and it is what I love most about being a shepherd. Lambing makes me feel the most alive of anything in the world! Yet, it can also be overly romanticized to folk who have never worked a full lambing season.

It can be a rough old life: up at the crack of a sparrow's fart, back to bed when the owl call echoes around the valley. Being out in the hills, and covered in dirt and yow's vaginal juice, my bones ache more with each year that passes. Meals are a luxury. Dinner – a reheated dish that has been frozen in advance for the yearly event – is likely to be at 10 p.m.. I mostly live off bread and consume buckets of tea and biscuits.

Showers are what happens when your dog shakes off a puddle. It's the last thing on your mind by the time you've taken off all your 15 layers of lambing gear. Taking boots off to go inside is a stretch too far. Some days your own body odour starts to compete with the surrounding farmyard smells and your sleeves are permanently rolled up ready to be elbow deep in a sheep's uterus to save a life at a moment's notice. You make friends with the local hedge as you spend more time pissing beside it than you do inside in an actual toilet. The clock on the wall becomes redundant for a month as you lose track of reality and the outside world!

Then, at the end of the day, as you slump into bed like a sack of spuds and the bleats of ewes and lambs fall quiet, content with full bellies, you remember why you do this… because, secretly, you love every minute, every filthy, achy, precious, joyful moment of it.

Lambing can be so busy, though. Weeks disappear like a song on the wind, but some moments stop you in your tracks. Once, as I drove through the rain on the quad at the crack of dawn, I saw that a yow had lambed in the night and, as I got to her, I noticed neither lamb had fed and both were dying. What took me aback the most is that the ewe knew it and let me help her without an ounce of fuss. These yows are wild and kick the hell out of you normally, but there was an understanding between us. An unspoken connection and, as I sat there after doing all I could to revive them, I thought, *this is why I do this* – willing them both to live, beating myself up for not being there sooner, but wrapping them all up in my arms and giving them all the love I could as the yow lamb passed over but the wether (boy) held on.

In moments like this, the world stands still and I can almost see through the veil. To encounter so much grief and so much joy in one day, one moment, is a lot to withstand. I swear I can feel a layer of flesh around my heart fall away as another loss fades. Imagine all that life and death passing through your spirit each day. I think this may be why shepherds are generally so intuitive – they are portals and the veil is always thin around them.

After about 30 minutes of sitting together and not moving, I brought the yow and her weak wether lamb back to the farm. Two days later, I returned them to the field and then every time I passed them on my rounds, we made eye contact with a subtle nod between us.

This shepherd's heart. This lambing life: brutal, gentle and full of love. There is no place I'd rather be. This is my medicine – lambing wild in nature.

I must have seen a thousand red sunsets, but I see every one of them as though it's my first. I often camp out over lambing and the sound of rain falling on the tent or the roof of the van are the Earth's melodical alarm to rise and tend the yows.

The truth is… when I go back to a house made of bricks, grateful and blessed as I am, it does not belong to me. I own very little and my world changes as I step through the door. I find the black cloud of depression has snuck in as I close the door, hiding in the cracks of the walls ready to weigh on me heavily as I sleep.

This is not my home. I am forever moving clutter around a house that I have little need for. I am severing my ties with the land as I sleep suspended, and not on the ground where my energy is recharged every night. Lying flat to the earth is when energies pass between soil and blood to renew body and mind. Then, connections are earthed and affirmed, and cells and fibres are fed by the invisible layer we all have that connects us to our home. Call it the force, the spirit, the transcendent veil – every night we're absent from our connection to the earth, we lose a little more of ourselves.

Tales from the Lambing Field

Lambing season can also bring more dramatic events, such as when a dog attacked my flock and one of my gorgeous girls was mauled in the attack. She was called Treasure, a lovely deep copper-coloured yow with white spots, and she was one of the first sheep I lambed in my flock. Her sister was called Anna and they were inseparable. In every one of the thousands of photos of my flock, they appear side by side. Treasure was in lamb when she was attacked by the out-of-control dog with a cowardly owner who didn't stick around to see if he could save my poor girl or ring for help. I lost both Treasure and her unborn lamb that day and Anna was by her body when I recovered her. Three days later, Anna was also dead. There were no physical wounds, but I called for a postmortem to rule out any transferable disease and the vet found that there had been distress to her heart and it was likely she had a cardiac arrest – a broken heart. Anna was also pregnant; I lost them all. So, I'll agree sheep are daft and clumsy and irritable and expensive at times, but no one will ever convince me they are thick and don't understand emotion.

This shepherd's
heart. This lambing
life: brutal, gentle
and full of love.
There is no place I'd
rather be. This is my
medicine – lambing
wild in nature.

I encountered another display of intelligence in Swaledales, quite possibly one of my favourite sheep breeds because the yows are stubborn wild betches! I like that in a female! Stories of catching yows would make a book in itself. Once I caught a yow that needed help and I was determined not to let go – we ended up rolling down the hill, both as stubborn as each other. I won! Swaledales are also fiercely protective mothers and, on one occasion, I saw a yow in the throes of labour right at the top of a hill, sheltered by a high stone wall. She had been going a while and I needed to get closer to check if she was okay. So, I turned off the quad engine and started to monkey crawl through the grass up to where she was lying and bearing down to push her lamb out.

The lapwings screeched above as I must have been close to their nest. The wind was bitter and I could understand why the lamb wanted to stay in that bubble of warm liquid for as long as possible. As I crept closer, the yow started to get nervous, so immediately, drawn up from some primal instinct in my belly, I started speaking in sheep language – a deep throated mutter, mutter, made by keeping my mouth closed but using my tonsils and throat to bleat like a lamb. This made the yow think she'd popped the lamb out, though she hadn't, so she started calling back to me. I continued muttering and crawling closer, with her returning my call. I ended up sitting right by her, lying down so as not to intimidate her, and she relaxed so much that her lamb came forth out into the falling light of that chilly spring day.

I felt all of life's tribulations ebb away as she began licking her lamb and clearing her airways of amniotic fluid. Not a soul witnessed this birth apart from me, the yow and a few lapwings who still had a beef with me for being too close to their chicks. The view was spectacular across the rolling green and heather-covered hills. The best part of the job right there.

Another example of the intelligence of sheep can be found in one of my oldest sheep, May. She is a real character, very clever and has learned to lie down on command! It's one of my favourite party tricks when folk come to visit the flock. But don't expect your average sheep out in the field with little human interaction to do this; it takes time, trust and love.

Take Your Time

Pace is important because if you do jobs at speed with sheep, it often causes them to become stressed and misbehave, for they frighten very easily. If they don't trust your motive, they will let you know about it. With sheep, you've got to earn their trust. Whether you have commercial units of thousands or just a few as pets, it's all the same theory. The animal needs to know you're not going to beat it for fidgeting while you're trying to administer a metal gun into its gullet to rid its digestive system of worms, or some other routine job you need to do to keep your flock in good shape. They only know how to read a situation by you and your body language, and if your signals are showing stress, the animal will feel it too. Take. Your. Time. Time is not money, but bad management will cause you to lose money. Take time to understand your animals and work with them and nature, the earth, soil, the seasons…. If you react against this idea and feel the slow approach is beneath you, then you're in the wrong business.

If you're trying to get sheep through a space and they won't budge, step back and they will acknowledge the space and walk on faster than if you try to shove them through with your knee or foot. The last farmer I worked with was amazed at the ease with which I got jobs done and how different the sheep were with me. He implements the same calmer practice now and it is better all round for him and the sheep. It's not rocket science, is it? Respect isn't just for humans – it's for everything with a heartbeat and a root.

We don't respect animals and nature because we see ourselves as separate from them. Sheep are now engrained in our evolutionary story, but they have not been part of that story for as long as wolves, bison, crows or whales, and look at how we destroy their spirits, history, habitats and reputations. We need them. Every single living being has a role, but we live in a world where patriarchal thinking conditions us to believe animals are a constant threat, not a benefit. Humans are the most dangerous species on the planet, yet we act as though the whole universe owes us something. We take, take, take and rarely give back. And if we do give back, it's only in the form of waste, chemicals and plastic. We burden the planet; we do not honour it. We treat our domesticated animals with even less respect and value. We do not fear sheep because we can control them. We cannot control wolves, and we are afraid of their spirit and power, so we destroy them. That is the way of modern man.

I believe that women generally view and treat the animal world differently. Sheep sense this. They behave differently with me than they do with a man, because sheep, like wolves, are threatened by those who seek to destroy them. The wolf is not afraid of the spirit of a woman, nor is the sheep. There are exceptions of course. Some women may become infected by a man's world, and adapt and evolve to fit in, while there are some men who are gentle, more considerate and in tune with animal behaviour. These are just my reflections based on personal experience.

If this idea makes you feel uncomfortable, it may be because it resonates with you on an unconscious level and it is a trigger to help you recognize and heal. Truth and light push out dark lies that dwell in the shadows. The only thing certain in life is change, and in order to change old ways, we must bring them into the light.

Dogs and Sheep

Sorry, I went off on a tangent when we're supposed to be talking about fluffy sheep! But I have another important side note – this time about dogs attacking sheep. After losing count of dog attacks over the years, I have become sick of seeing shepherds having to pick up the pieces, literally, in some cases. It needs to be understood that every dog will chase or attack a sheep when it runs. It's a game and sometimes the sheep become prey. A sheep does not have to sustain physical wounds for it to drop dead. Merely 'worrying' a sheep may cause a yow to abort her lambs or cardiac arrest and death.

These incidents are devastating when you've spent years raising a flock and moulding a particular bloodline across several generations. Apart from this, the sheep are my family, so any loss is not only financial; it's devastating. Sheep are not a commodity to me, they're my daily life, my every day. I know each one by name and I work tirelessly to keep them safe, but I can't be there 24/7. Although I have begged people to keep their dogs on leads, it's futile as most dog owners do not consider that a moment of freedom for their dog can cause a lifetime of trauma for sheep and shepherd. Irresponsible dog owners are not only putting my animals at risk, they may be endangering their dog as well, because farmers are within their rights to kill a dog that is worrying livestock. Leads are a valuable tool – use them.

Regenerative Agriculture

There are now many incredible farms giving animals and nature a fighting chance to live their best life possible. I'm so proud to support regenerative agriculture by moving away from outdated practices, learning from Indigenous farming cultures and using these methods to care for the land, the crops and the animals we use to manage the land, in order to feed the nation. There's been a real shift over the last 20 years as society has seen the damage caused to our bodies and natural habitats by the overuse of pesticides and chemicals.

There is a movement of change that is intent on bringing back insect and bird species from the brink of extinction, saving habitats at the edge of being lost forever, and seeking to alleviate chronic human diseases that are spiralling upwards at an alarming rate. Our guts are damaged and the only way we can reverse this is through the land, through the care we give our soil and by replacing minerals to the earth. We know what needs to be done, but those who have the answers need to be heard and funded to implement the changes so desperately needed right now.

They say there is only a generation's worth of harvest left in UK soil before it is dead. One day I long for my own land so that I can care for and give her what's needed to bring her back to life. I have been searching for years, but if you're a poor shepherd and not from farming stock or the aristocracy, you've got more chance of braiding yoghurt than you have of gaining any land in the UK! Access to land to feed your family and community used to be a basic right in this country and world. Half of England is owned by less than 1 per cent of the population – that makes me shudder. Figures show that if the land was distributed evenly, each person would have just over half an acre and that would mean we could be reliant on ourselves and not a centralized government. Need I say more?

CHAPTER 8

The Yorkshire Dales

There was a particularly special farm I worked on in Nidderdale, in the Yorkshire Dales, which belonged to David and Judy Middlemiss. You know those places where you leave a piece of your heart? Well, Coville House Farm was one such place. I drove down the narrow lanes past fields lined with stone walls and sheep to arrive at the farm. As I ventured out onto the land, I lay down invisible roots. It felt like I had come home; I belonged here. It is a hill farm that sits among the heather and the peat-covered bogs of the Yorkshire Dales. The banks of the farm brush against Gouthwaite Reservoir. Rich populations of curlews and lapwings, grouse and hen harrier thrive there, and Swaledale sheep blanket the hills. As I've already said, the Swaledale is one of my favourite sheep breeds. I love their attitude; they are wild and stubborn and rarely do what you expect or beg them to do, depending how badly you need them to move. Yet most folk dislike them for the exact reasons I love them. If they didn't have these qualities, they wouldn't survive the harshness the hills bring in winter. I worked on Coville House Farm for several years while Harry was growing up. It was the perfect place to raise a child and I longed to live there and give Harry the life I could only have dreamed of when I was growing up. We didn't get to live there permanently, but I worked as much as I could and we stayed in our little caravan between school terms and Harry's trips to his dad.

The opportunity to work on this farm came about through a mutual friend. I was invited to visit the farm, and on arrival David showed me around and took me straight up into the hills on his quad bike. This was the first time I'd ever been on a hill farm, or seen a sheepdog work so powerfully, and I was smitten by it all. I was a child of the eighties and grew up loving *All Creatures Great and Small* by James Herriot, and the TV show based on this series of books, so it was magical to see that those places actually existed in real life, not just the fairy tale of my imagination. The Middlemiss's dog, Bett, was extraordinary. We sat on the quad bike at the top of the moor and watched her round up several hundred sheep without a single command from her master. She glanced at him occasionally to gain comfort from his nod that she was bringing them together in the right way, but generally she just knew what to do – her instincts were strong.

The quad engine hummed in the background, as I stood in awe at the view that stretched out before me. Picture this: fields of golden green, with trees lining the gullies that snaked down to the valley bottom, carved out by ice-cold brown water, coloured from the peat bogs through which it filtered, falling gently across boulders and velvet ferns as it coursed to the reservoir below. The sun kissed the horizon and beams shot out across the landscape and up into the pink sky, which lit up the sheep peppered across the fields on the far side of the valley. It all took my breath away and I knew in that moment that I belonged here in these hills, surrounded by sheep and sunsets and the cool evening breeze. 'Lie down lass', David called to Bett as her job was done. He told me, 'If I go home now and don't come back until the morning, she'll still be there. She won't move from that spot.' *I want a dog just like her one day*, I thought to myself. Then, 18 months later Bett gave birth to 13 pups! Only nine survived but within that bunch of fur and funny pink noses was the girl who would become my lifelong companion through the rest of my shepherding life. (More on her in the next chapter.)

Yorkshire Grit

I have never worked in such a harsh, unforgiving yet staggeringly beautiful environment. I remember one Saturday morning, it was 5 a.m. and there was a blizzard, a proper whiteout, and I was heading back down the fell with David. We were bouncing down the gravel track and David came to a halt on his quad and turned to me to say, 'Is there really nothing else a young lass like you would rather be doing on a Saturday morning?' I knew all my friends would be tucked up in bed after going out the night before… but I pulled my scarf away from my face, wiped the snow piling up around my eyes, and with a beaming smile replied, 'No!! This is exactly where I want to be.' I've never been happier than I was then.

I worked mostly alone in the hills, lambing outdoors and doing all the other jobs required of a shepherd throughout the year on a hill farm. It's not a nine-to-five job, it's a way of life. Believe me when I tell you my body suffered up there, but my mind was the most alive it's ever been. I witnessed some of the most extraordinary behaviours from those hardy, tough animals. I shared my sunsets with lapwings, curlews, little owls and so many more, who flew for me every time I was out in the wild with them alone… a spectacle just for me. I had no need to share it with the world.

You have to be physically tough, fit and strong for this work. You have to know there will be times when you're going to get hurt and no one will be around to rescue you. You need to have grit, to dig deep, through times of extreme cold and when you are drenched through for hours on end, but you have to keep searching for a sheep, walking for miles, trudging through mud, working in the dark and having to overcome extreme bouts of fear, hunger and despair. Many times, I've been alone and heard noises when sleeping out on the hill or in my caravan far away from civilisation. You know when you sense something is there… but you're too scared to move.

There are times when you've got to have discipline to get out of your cosy bed. I'd often get dressed in bed to avoid facing the cold shock of stripping away the cosy sheets in temperatures of minus 10 degrees. When lambing for weeks on end, your body aches in places you didn't know existed! But most of all, you relish the privilege of being the gate-keeper of the veil, the portal between life and death.

This way of life is as close as I'll get to being wild, free and actually learning to survive in the great outdoors. Dealing with life and death every day tests your resolve; the veil is very thin and you walk a tight rope of winning and losing and carrying on, through the blood, sweat and tears. The life and harshness of the elements stirs something primal in you, reminiscent of a time when there was no escape back to towns and technology; when this was it. With no central heating, you had to toil to make a fire before hypothermia sets in. But your immune system and resilience becomes strong when you are constantly battling the weather and tiredness. When

I die, I want to lie down in the long grasses, dissolve into the peat bogs and rocky pools, and let my body be picked over by crows and hawks. Let the dung beetles, worms and weevils feast and the sheep nibble the grass that grows over what remains. Let the last thing I see be the stars making way for the moon to open her arms and welcome me back into the core of Mother Earth. May the dust of my bones forever drift across the wild moorlands of the Yorkshire Dales and if you see a spirit up there wandering those hills after I am gone, look out for the black wolf trailing behind and you'll know it is me.

Endings

Then suddenly, one day, after being immersed in that life and landscape for several years, it all ended. I remember my final sunset in that land as I watched a Swaledale yow and her newborn lamb disappear over the hill and into the dusk. I did not imagine that this would mark the end of a big chapter in my life. I packed my dogs and bags, left my cosy caravan where it stood and never returned.

Six years later, I was asked to lamb on another hill farm in the Yorkshire Dales. It happened to be just a stone's throw from Coville House Farm. Something tugged at my gut to contact David and Judy while I was there, to see how they were and whether the farm was still working. I was so pleased to get a reply asking me to go for a brew between lambing duties. The route across those moors took me back and I felt a lump in my throat as I approached the old lane that took me up to the farmhouse. Sadly, they farmed no more. The sheep had gone, the land was about to be sold and David, after having several strokes and now dementia, didn't have long on this Earth. But the glint in his eye when I walked in told me he remembered me. We sat and reminisced for a while and as I drove away, knowing that was the last time I'd see him, I hope he knew how much happiness he, those wild sheep and that enchantingly beautiful farm brought me. You see, when you're a farmer, you're a farmer for life. You're born of a different breed; the blood runs differently in your veins and the story is as old as the hills. When the shepherd stops, so does the heart.

The day after I finished writing this chapter, it was Samhain. The time when the cailleach, known as the old crone or hag in Celtic mythology, as the bringer of winter brought with her an eerie fog which hovered across the land. Out from the mist a barn owl came flying straight towards me. She looked me in the eye and banked left sharply, flying around me in a very close circle before landing on a nearby post. The owl is the bringer of news, sometimes death, or death of a chapter in life. She brought both. Two hours later, I received a message that David had died and with him that part of my life closed. Grief and letting go. The birds bring the messages if you're willing to receive them.

So, what I'm trying to say is, moments and circumstances can change in our lives without choice or warning. When they are gone, good or bad, they are gone. See the good and beauty in every moment. If things are negative, find the positive. If there are cracks, mend them; if there are unresolved issues, share them. When you wake tomorrow, if things you love and invest in had changed or ended, what would you miss? Live in the now and don't regret a single day.

CHAPTER 9

Kes

Kes, my first border collie, my first sheepdog, was born in Yorkshire, at Coville House Farm. My right-hand girl – the most intelligent, gentle creature I know. What adventures I have had with the little lassie. She is now nine years old and I know I'll never own another dog like her. She is the first dog I have trained and we've both just winged it. She carries me daily with her spirit…. All our trials and tribulations are dealt with together; when I'm weak, she is strong. When I'm strong, she listens. It just works. There have been times when I have reached my limit, when I've tried several times to round up a flock of awkward sheep. This usually happens on a full moon, when a lot seems to go wrong – they jump walls, split up, run the wrong way, hurdles fall over – and I've thrown in the towel and collapsed in a mardy heap on the floor with a sigh and a few expletives. When this happens, Kes looks at me and knows I'm done. As I sit there, head in hands, she disappears off into the distance to do all the work of rounding up the sheep, quietly and calmly, and brings them to the gate I need them to go through. She glances at me as if to say, 'There you go, Mam.'

She teaches me the lesson that sometimes we just need to get out of our own way!

On one occasion she helped avert a major disaster, and we added Emergency Animal Rescue to her list of qualities! Harry and I were off Christmas-tree hunting in the woods. As we approached a railway line, passing by a livestock market on the left, I saw some sheep and thought, *How odd, I've never seen them out grazing before on the grass in front; normally they are in pens ready for tomorrow's market.* Then I quickly realized that the sheep were heading out into the road, across the car park and towards the railway line. I pulled over in the truck with Kes in the back and leapt out like a mad woman, yelling to Harry to go and get help.

The road was packed with traffic, because it was a very busy market town and on a Friday afternoon the hazards were endless. Kes knew exactly what I was thinking. We got to work, but after several frantic moments of weaving between traffic and speeding cars, chasing erratic sheep (one was even blind, which made me question who was leading who), I realized it was too dangerous. I called Kes back and managed to push most of the sheep into the market field single handedly, while everyone (apart from Harry, who was trying to rugby tackle the blind ewe) watched with great enthusiasm. Cheers for the help! After we averted what can only be described as a major incident, Kes rounded the sheep back up and into the market pens. Never a dull moment!

We have long had close bonds with our animal relatives and created countless stories of our animal kin through folklore, mythology and songs of old. The wolf helped us hunt, the birds warned us of danger with their alarm cries, and the whales and dolphins spoke their great wisdom out of the oceans and carried people being tossed about on the waves to the safety of the shore. My bond with the animals I commune with today is no different; the sheepdogs live to please me and be praised.

Have you ever had an animal whose soul feels ancient, as if it has been here before? I feel this with Kes. She has helped guide me down the ancient path of shepherding – an ancient occupation, one that I feel I walked a thousand years ago. If a dog could talk, she'd be the gentlest of grandmothers, softly herding her offspring and sheep across the hills and valleys of the Earth. She sees me at my weakest, my most vulnerable, through my rage at the world and my sadness, yet she does not leave my side. The most loyal of creatures I've ever encountered, it's as if she knows I need her and would be lost without her – she is the guide that never falters. I often have nightmares and she knows this and wakes me to snuggle into my chest. We are both mothers bound by an invisible thread.

I look at her now, ageing into her 10th year, and I see her starting to slow down. I know this season of working together will be our last and best adventure. I am terrified of her death, but I know the universe provides the comfort we need at the right time. So, another Kes will come, maybe not in animal form, but she will come, and I will keep watch for her out on the rolling green hills and heather-covered moors of the land we both love most.

CHAPTER 10

Red Sky at Night

When you're a shepherd, red sky at night doesn't always bring delight.

5 a.m. in the hills, battling a blizzard to bring the flock down to shelter.

When weekends, birthdays and Christmases don't exist.

Where skin ages twice as fast and hair blows wild in the wind, laden with leaves and hay.

Clothes without dirt and holes and worn-out patches are a thing of the past.

Isolation and weariness where only the birds and bogs bring comfort and company.

A life that offers mud as make-up, injuries you must ignore and money that is only earned to pay for the next bag of feed or repair to the truck.

Sleeping deeply in bursts merely to count more sheep.

Where weakness is tested with wounds from the endless battles to tackle and catch the strays or injured, or that one sheep that never follows the crowd.

Where your closest ally is your dog who will never leave your side through fight or flight.

To witness birth in such startling and humbling ways.

To endure pain to bring food for the family and feed the many.

To battle an industry that still sees the female sex as weak.

To bring hope and light to the most sustainable yet undervalued material – wool – that once created a thriving industry on our shores.

Why?

Because we love every second. It's all worth it and nothing is wasted. We share sunrises and sunsets with animals we love while most people are tucked up in bed and miss it all. To sit in the darkness and watch the shadows fall across pastures and hills is one of the greatest privileges ever bestowed upon someone. To share such a life with our children; to pass knowledge and skills on to those in the next generation who are willing to take up the role. We have resilience and determination beyond our years. We don't all do it in the same way – every shepherd has a different way. But those who truly shepherd have hearts that beat to the same rhythm. Our feet walk an ancient path with great honour and responsibility, and we do it with pride and love for an animal who is one of the most abundant on our living Earth. These sheep shape our landscape and my heart.

PART II

Rediscovering
Our Origins

This year, I discovered that my name in Old Irish (Eílís Ní Chnáimhsighe) translates to midwife and bone setter. I use tools, skills and ancient wisdom to make a difference in this world. These tools are given to all of us by the Great Mother, through a catalogue of experiences and trials in life. She chooses us to be portals for the truth and she uses me like a hollow bone through which messages come from animals and the otherworld.

I'm here to be a vessel for the truth, so the spirit can work through me to fulfil her purpose. In this section, I recount all my experiences demonstrating this belief, including the discovery of an ancient craft that is about death and rebirth, a continual cycle of life and renewal, bringing back the spirit of the animal through the hide and what wool has taught us about survival and longevity.

CHAPTER 11

Mother

My mother sacrificed her life to raise four children alone and with no support. She worked four jobs while raising us on home-cooked fresh food, with discipline and love. I have my spirit and passion for life now because of my mother. I also thank her for my gift of dance. She will be the first to admit that she and my father got many things wrong in parenting, but they are human beings living in the shadow of their own traumatic upbringings, which were void of nurture and affection. Nothing in this book is meant to degrade either of my parents. They may not have always done their best, but they did strive to give us what we most needed and to raise us to adulthood; I honour my mother the most for that achievement.

We've all been fucked up by our childhoods in one way or another. We tend to remember the bad and forget the good. You can spend your whole life blaming your upbringing or your parents for the way you are: for the way you fail at tasks, treat others like crap, can't hold down a job or relationship. But there comes a point, when you become an adult, when you must choose to forgive the damaging aspects of your childhood; forgive even if you don't want to and stop blaming others for your inadequacies, mistakes and failures. I share your grief in the loss of a childhood or a support network to fall on when things don't go to plan. But becoming an adult means letting go of the pain of the past. Your future will not wait for you to spend years in psychotherapy or meditation. It will just fly and pass you by and you'll wind up with little time left to start living because you're still carrying the baggage that does not heal that agony in your heart; it only weighs you down.

I internally thank both of my parents for bringing me into the world and working hard to provide for me so that I could reach adulthood and make a new life. I grieved for many years about the hardships I faced, then I closed the chapter of my childhood. I didn't see my father for many years and many traumatic things happened to me growing up, but those things do not define me – they are lessons to help me be the parent I am now. In order to heal we *must* let go of that which eats away at us and starves us of a future free of guilt, shame and sadness. Through choosing to forgive my father, together we crossed the bridges of stubbornness and pride. In his final years on this Earth, I couldn't have loved anyone more than my father, and my son had a closer bond with his grandfather than I ever had with him when growing up. So, no matter how deep the scar, I believe if you're willing to take responsibility for your own life and decisions in adulthood and let that past pain go, you can heal generational wounds and they will not continue in your line.

I do recognize that some wounds are too deep and no matter the blood bonds, some bridges cannot be rebuilt. But you can still refuse to allow that damage to influence the rest of your life – don't give it that power. Scream out your pain, find a bridge somewhere or a mountain top, and holler out the cry from the depths of your soul, so loud and powerful that you wake the sleeping dragons of the fairy-tale world. The release you will feel from doing this can be more effective than years spent sitting in a therapy chair. It's primal and oh-so healing. Do anything you need to, but do not carry that pain forwards into your future.

The Community We Crave

When we lived in communities and tribal nations, our social structure was very different. You only need to look at the remaining Indigenous clans peppered across the world to see how they live and create balance and order. The women live and gather together. They go to each other for most of their needs and the men play a different role – in reproduction and supporting what the women create. The man's role is as essential as the woman's role, but they know their roles and don't try to heal problems they're not made to tackle.

If you're in a challenging relationship right now and you're looking to your partner to fulfil that gaping wound in your soul, I promise, from experience, that you'll only ever clash because you expect something they simply don't have the tools to give. And in the pursuit of affirmation from them, you only further diminish and give away your power by being reliant on them for your emotional needs. At the same time, they may also become emasculated because they're trying to fulfil a role for which they're not equipped. We often look to others for healing, but the only way you will heal from anything in life is by walking through the fire alone; the only constant force that will hold you up is not your parents, best friends, partner or spouse, but nature. Named *saoiera* in the Mohawk language, nature is represented as Grandmother Moon, the ocean and dirt.

Across the Generations

It is not just the neediness of our wounded hearts through physical and mental trauma that causes us to come up against roadblocks in this life, but our spirits give us warnings too. I had many reasons not to trust men in my youth, but that was nothing compared to the uncontrollable reaction my spirit had in adulthood when faced with the patriarchy and misogyny. There was a trigger – my spirit recognized the darkness in their line from the experiences of women in my line. I am talking about the massacre of witches. Women carry a witch wound and it may be affecting you in ways you don't even recognize, but it's possible to heal from it.

Every woman and man in your line who has passed on generational trauma did not have the wisdom or knowledge or, most importantly, the heart to stop it. If you decide the buck stops with you, then you need to *feel* all of it and it's going to hurt. You have to do the work! Go out into the wild somewhere safe, and from the depths of your belly speak out and acknowledge the root of the trauma, honour its teaching but refuse to feed it any more. Then, grieve its loss. Cry it out alone in nature, only tell the bark of the Great Grandmother Oak *(see page 212)*. Sit beneath her boughs and whisper your plan and I promise she will help you as she helped me.

Some believe that we carry the weight of learned behaviour from conflict and depression, as well as what we see and what we *cannot* see. This includes all that your ancestors witnessed during their lifetime, be it poverty, abuse, murder, loneliness or abandonment. You will share these feelings, too; empaths suffer deeply in this way. I decided it would stop with me and when Harry was born, I declared to the universe that I would try my best to prevent my damage and pain being projected onto him and his new, fragile, magic-filled mind of wonder. He was a new book, a new song who I would protect at all costs from anger and bitterness.

I am paddling the stormy waters every day, as I know we all are. I also know that I am born for this time and I believe every woman on Earth now is born to take up the reins of our sacred female ancestors. We need to remember that we are the portal between life and death. We are the life-givers who bring great healing and change for our children. We are remembering and rising to the words of our grandmothers. We need their wisdom and guidance now more than ever.

Parenthood

No one ever has a manual on parenting… but parenting through the storms and truly loving your child means making a choice not to hand on your ancestral damage. Instead, show them the solar system, make fire with them and embark on adventures together. Teach them to love themselves before others, to believe in the Great Spirit and how to care for Mother Earth. Learned behaviour will be their biggest memory, so you must guide them through this wilderness of life with care.

I have got parenting wrong many times, and still do. I'm neurotic about my son's whereabouts, even though he moved out four years ago and is almost 21. I think it's natural and I know most mothers feel like this because it is so alien to be apart from our children, no matter their age. There is an invisible umbilical cord that spans across the globe and reaches them wherever they are, so that when they are in need, distress, upset or in trouble, we feel it before we hear about it.

Although I will always be a mother, raising children is finite and does end. In the blink of an eye, he is not a boy, but a young man. I felt grief when Harry left; the house fell deathly quiet. We had such adventures together, my little shadow and I: from lambing together across the country to our epic trek to Fairisle, one of the most remote islands in the British Isles; from camping to road tripping; from raising our beloved dogs together to making memories of all kinds to reminisce over. Some of your greatest memories are made when you least expect it.

It was September on the Isle of Skye, and we were staying in a quaint little croft offered to me as a holiday in exchange for a sheepskin I made. That's my idea of trading goods! We had been settling down for the evening after a harsh, cold and wet day when I had this urge to get in the car and go. I said: 'Harry, I know, let's go and see the Old Man of Storr.' I knew the tourists would have gone and I wanted to experience this mythical place alone with my son, surrounded only by the rocks, wind and heavy spirit-filled clouds.

We had little time before darkness fell so our pace was quick. When you're on a mission, it's incredible where the strength in your legs comes from…. You dig deep to push on as the horizon keeps slipping away as the light falls. The Old Man of Storr kept teasing us through the passing haze, 'Come on now dear, courage… I'm waiting.' I looked up and smiled. An old man, my father's face in his towering stature, encouraged me on.

I arrived a few steps behind Harry and as we stood there, the wind howling around our cheeks, taking in the view of the beautiful islands beyond, a silence fell, so eerie but peaceful. We stopped and looked at each other just knowing…. In that moment, you could have heard a pin drop and the Great Spirit of life and the power of

Mother Nature's enchanting beauty was more powerful and present than I ever remember. We breathed her in, a sacred memory formed for a lifetime.

Harry is my blood, my flesh, my soul, my heart and I am proud of his spirit. I adore all that he is, but what life awaits him? I can only guide and nurture him until he finds his own path. I wrote this letter to Harry as I lay in a hospital bed in 2019, believing I wouldn't make it through the night. The words came deep from a mother's heart and I share it with you to encourage any mothers and fathers out there to share their hearts with their own children:

Dream Harry. Have dreams. Think of them every day then I promise they will manifest into your life.

You are my gift to the world and I love you.

Make your life count, Harry.

Keep always connected to nature and Mother Earth. She will feed you. Grandma Moon will protect you and the universe will carve out your path and you must follow it.

Believe in your outstanding qualities and skills. Believe you can make a difference in this world.

Swim against the tide, remember to question everything. Don't accept all rules and embrace change.

See beyond the surface, because what lies beneath holds your true purpose and destiny in this world.

Make your life count, Harry.

The day after you were born, I got up at sunrise and took you down to the sea.... I held you to the sun and showed you to her and the sky and the moon. I was so proud and I asked that she'd always look after you. And I know she will, until she returns you to me.

We will always be together, in each and every realm and life. We are forever entwined. You're a part of me and I'm a part of you, always, forever and to eternity.

CHAPTER 12

Owl

One winter's morning, at sunrise, a beautiful tawny owl brought herself to me, in need of love and rehabilitation. A bird messenger of great medicine, it was a dream encounter to restore her life and help her heal.

Luna

I was driving to check the sheep and must have been distracted by something because I missed the turning into the field completely, so continued on to turn around at the end of the road. Why did I look right, at another entrance to the arable fields? You normally look straight ahead when driving, but I looked right, and down on the ground, sitting in a gateway, was a tawny owl. I'd travelled a good few metres past the owl, so I reversed and it was still there, alive but motionless – a beautiful tawny owl with a rare grey-morph colouring to her feathers. I was able to pick her up in a towel and assess her condition. I could tell she was thin and barely moving, so I took her home and spent the next three months learning how to raise and rehabilitate a wild bird.

She had been living in an area where there was fierce competition for food and her parents may have died while raising her as she was still young. I learned so much during that time and we became very close. I named her Luna. She went everywhere with me and even though she was a feisty little madam, she never harmed me intentionally, but those razor-sharp talons scratched my hands on several occasions. I wasn't the only one to fall in love with her. She amassed quite a following of her own on social media and the donations for her care were so heart-warming. Three months felt like three years, and I was torn between setting her free and wishing to keep her with me in captivity. She had not been raised by her parents and taught how to hunt, although we did practise, and she became a constant companion on my arm; I couldn't imagine life without her. But if I've learned anything about love, in particular loving animals, I know we must love them and let them go, for they do not belong to us. Luna (aka 'teet-owl') came not long after my father died and she was the distraction I needed to help me in my grief. Life has taught me that only by letting go, no matter how painful that is, can we bring in what's waiting for us. It's the only way we can see what is waiting behind the next door. Suffering makes you recognize when something is not meant for you, and finding the courage to allow it to die is the first big step to trusting and loving ourselves and our purpose.

The spirit of the owl symbolizes:

- intuition and the ability to see what others do not see
- the capacity to see beyond deceit and masks
- wisdom
- change
- death (usually a symbolic one, like a life transition)

We must break the psychological chains when letting go or we will forever be trapped in a no man's land of emotional stagnation – never moving forwards into our potential, but held back by regret and heartache.

I returned Luna to the wild, where I wish I could have followed her! I asked her to visit me again and for the moon to help her hunt, and off she flew into the velvet black night. That night, I had a bad dream. As I lay awake at 4 a.m., I heard a 'twit twoooo' from the tree outside my bedroom window. I smiled and my eyes leaked as I thought, *she's coming to thank me.* That was enough for me to fully let her go, not just physically but by severing the tie to my heart. We must break the psychological chains when letting go or we will forever be trapped in a no man's land of emotional stagnation – never moving forwards into our potential, but held back by regret and heartache.

Luna was the first wild bird I had rescued and returned to the wild. After her, they started coming in floods: the barn owls, buzzards and kestrels and many more messenger birds. I guess the spirit world knew the flood gates had opened, so threw the healing thick and fast my way.

Hushwing

Hushwing was another owl, a barn owl, who also stole a piece of my heart. Barn owls are incredible birds. Mostly relying on sound to locate their prey, they fly low and slowly, back and forth across hunting grounds before diving to catch and eat their prey whole. They can't digest fur or bones, so regurgitate these in pellets. Their feathers are serrated, which makes them silent hunters, able to catch their prey undetected. The barn owl is the most ghostly, comforting form of a guide I've ever witnessed. She is now my constant companion, from living in my downstairs toilet to appearing above my head when grief fills my heart. The barn owl is never far from me.

The thing about death – in every form, no matter how much you prepare for it and learn through suffering to expect it – is that it robs you of the moments you'll never get back. You may wish you could halt time and give a loved one one more kiss, or tell them how much happiness they've brought you. I have learned so much about death from having animals in my care, but I can't help but feel like I've failed every time I lose one. Before the arrival of each death, my intuition told me it was coming. The signs are there to prepare us, they bring messages of knowledge, if only we can see them and interpret an ancient wisdom almost lost to our civilized world.

I recently stopped bleeding for two months due to a hormonal illness and I began to grieve in case I was entering early menopause and would never see my blood again. I spent a full day, from 5 a.m. until 6 p.m., writing about blood. It was one day before the full moon, not just any full moon, a full moon in my sun sign, Taurus and a partial lunar eclipse. I went to the bathroom at 6:30 p.m. and shrieked in excitement, 'I'm bleeding!!!!' Never have I been so pleased to see blood. Immediately, I went out into the garden, the full moon shining in my eyes across the trees at the bottom of my garden. I held the blood in my hands up to her and thanked her over and over, and I tasted the sweet iron rich medicine on my lips. From a tree just a few metres away, a single female tawny owl called out and I just smiled like that was normal. It's not, of course. It's magic and Luna came into my mind: I bet it was her. When you step out of the confines of normality – to be brazen and bold, to be different – you will be rewarded.

Two days after this, one day after the full moon (which is acknowledged as including two days either side of its full phase), I went out in the evening to check the sheep. The flash of white in my peripheral alerted me to the far hedgerow where I saw, in all his glory, Hushwing dancing back and forth, rotating his wings on the hunt for food. I felt we noticed each other, the solar system reflected in his black eyes, as he banked then plummeted onto the ground a few metres away to gather a feast he had captured and previously nibbled. Without a sign, he lifted back up and away into the distance with the setting sun. I took a deep breath, my witchy senses tingling at the thrill of seeing him again – and such timing.

CHAPTER 13

The Seer

We forget how to recognize signs these days, how to read dreams. In the days of Boudicca, there were sub-groups within British tribes (such as the Iceni and Trinovantes) called 'the dreamers', who had been given the special gift from the gods of being able to read dreams. I can interpret about half of my dreams, but the other half are always a mystery that would need to be explained to me by an elder or a mentor. But these dreams sadly get lost as I have neither elder nor mentor, although I long for one.

Sensing the Signs

It's very easy to miss signs in dreams or in nature if we're not looking, or if our eyes are closed to the spirit world. We forget that we are not just a physical body, but have a spirit and a soul that have been here long before our physical selves. Many cultures, tales and mythologies speak of 'the seer,' who is in touch with their spirit and soul, and can bring messages from the underworld as a result. Some may think this is 'fairy talk'. Maybe you are one of them, but you should still be aware of the spirit and soul of other people and objects. Everything carries a spirit; every possession you own and thing you carry in life has a consequence or a benefit, so carefully consider what you hang on to and what you put out into the world. If you wish bad upon others, it will only bring bad vibes into your own life. If you acquire an object that once belonged to another, such as from a charity shop, it will bring its former owner's soul into your life. Be wiser about the things you invest in and if you can't get rid of them, burn herbs to rid them of negativity and stagnant energy. Say ceremonies over the past that still eats away at you and go out, barefoot, onto the cold dewy grass just before dawn and look up at the stars. I love speaking with Venus, who seems to shine brighter when I feel good, too. Ask Venus to send you the messengers.

As I write, Skye, my youngest sheepdog, has detected a presence; she is growling and staring into the distance; she sees something I can't. Do you have a sixth sense, a gut feeling that means you sense something happening before it happens? A flash in the corner of your eyes; goosebumps when something deep resonates with you; a high-pitched frequency in your ear; a prompt to look up, take note of your surroundings, await the sign? These spiritual messages, and many more, are all powers that we hold within us, but we've forgotten how to recognize and use them. Only with practice and ancient wisdom and ritual can we retrain ourselves to live more in the spirit world. At Samhain (Halloween) – when the bone woman archetype slithers among the mist and moss and the veil is at its thinnest – speak with her and your ancestors; ask them for protection and speak your gratitude and dreams into their ears.

Buzzards

When hardships come, the universe is clearing a path, and she sends messengers ahead to journey with you and make preparations. Buzzards have always been strong messenger birds for me. Making themselves visible and present in times of change or uncertainty, they cross my path and bring confirmation that I am going in the right direction. On the wings of buzzards, soaring high above the treetops, is where our spirits wait for us to reclaim them.

Not long after releasing Hushwing the owl, I found an injured buzzard in the hedgerow. Sadly, it became clear that she was too far gone. Her organs had already started to shut down and, underneath her feathers, she was skin and bone; I was maybe a day too late. I watched this majestic bird fading away, the haze of death emerging in her eyes. I held her close as she flew from this realm, and I felt as though I took on some of her spirit as she passed. A year later, another buzzard lives in my old dog cage in the kitchen. He came to me with a broken wing after being hit by a car. After six weeks of rehabilitation, I am almost ready to release this magical messenger bird back into the wild. I may not be able to save the world, but by saving this beautiful bird I can heal a small corner of it.

So much of our wildlife is struggling due to hunger and loss of habitat, but the buzzard has been one of our greatest native wildlife success stories, returning to flourish since their huge decline prior to the 1970s. I've seen them a thousand times, straining my neck upwards to get a glimpse as they soar overhead; my son calling them into the woodland when he was younger and the birds actually coming. There are countless photos on my camera of a blur in the sky; I know I will never capture their beauty, but I still try anyway. Once, I was searching for my sheep, walking miles in the wrong direction, when a buzzard flew past and called to me. I followed her and almost a kilometre (about half a mile) later, there were the sheep.

Feathers and Smoke

It is a rare treasure to find buzzard feathers scattered around the meadows and woodlands, and I collect them with pride. The First Nations people of Turtle Island believe that when you are going through a hard time or have a problem, if a feather appears on your path, then you will be blessed with spiritual support and guidance. You must accept this feather and use it as a smudging item in your smoke prayers. The spirit that dwells in this feather will come to you as your guide to help you with your problems and will protect you from harm. This powerful medicine will become one with you and spiritual gifts will manifest within you from the attributes of this feather. For you will now be able to summon this spirit guide whenever you use the sacred feather in your smoke prayers. You can also hang it on your window for protection from bad medicine. Whenever a bird places a part of itself in your path, the spirit of that bird has been asked to be your spirit guide for what lies ahead.

HOW TO USE A FEATHER IN SMOKE PRAYERS

1. Take the feather that has been left for you, or one you find meaning with, and cover it in the cleansing smoke of sage, cedar pine or any herb that's precious to you and burns well in a smudge.

2. Wrap the feather stem in leather cordage and add jewels, beads, crystals or shells that are important to you along the cord. Use

just the single feather or add a few together in a fan shape and bind the quills at the base with the leather.

3. This sacred, embellished flyer is now your ceremonial companion when communing with the goddesses of the universe and your messenger birds. Use the feather to wave over the burning candles and herbs, as you speak from your heart of gratitude.

◇◇◇◇◇◇◇◇◇◇◇◇◇◇◇◇◇◇

Other birds with specific associations include the heron, which is a sign of enduring patience – the change will come but hold your nerve. In Celtic folklore and mythology, ravens are associated with the goddess Morrigan, who represents death and war, and guards the natural environment. In Welsh mythology, ravens and crows are associated with the warrior god Brân the Blessed. Ravens gained mythical status as the mediators of life and death by consuming the flesh of dead animals.

CHAPTER 14

Turtle's Back

The name I was given at birth, my English name, is Elizabeth. That name carried me for 40 years until it faded with the sunset and with the wind when I was reborn into a new life, with a new name and a new quest. However, the name Elizabeth is still used by those who can't pronounce Iekawehatie (*yeah-ga-weh-ha-jay*) – meaning 'she paddles along', because I had crossed the great waters to find myself upon Turtle Island. The Kanienkeha'ka (Mohawk) people do not have a common singular, repetitive name. Instead, each child is born with a song. No one else is given that song and it will be their name from their day of birth, which is a 'happening' – a moment when nature declares how the child shall be remembered. Wahiakeron (*why-a-gearoo*), my elder's name, means 'apples on the ground'.

Have you ever taken a big risk, one that you didn't regret, but that changed the course of your life? Well, I took a big risk by selling most of my flock and following my heart to Canada to stay in the longhouses of the Kanienkeha'ka.

Life is about stepping out of your comfort zone because, beyond the bubble in which we exist lies a reality, a truth that few dare to seek and even fewer venture into. This life isn't a rehearsal, it's our chance to make things right before it's too late.

Looking back, I can see that every moment of my life had been leading to me travelling to Canada. Every day of my life, I dreamed of such a time when I'd encounter these people I longed to meet, and embrace all their wisdom, knowledge, teachings, history, purpose, law, connections, vision and hope. The fire in my spirit never died, but my mind and body almost gave up hope. You cry out one last time....

One Morning

It was an early spring morning, the sun glowing on the cobweb-filled windows as I tried to distract myself from every job in the house that needed doing before my son came back from visiting his father. Some days, when there are so many things that demand my attention – work, tax returns, cleaning the bathroom, patching the hole in the fence – I wander aimlessly, never able to focus on any of the tasks because my mind doesn't recognize this way of living. I'm stuck in ancient times with old blood.

The questions that flood my mind the second I wake up in the morning: *How do I escape the trappings of this estate I live on where neighbours constantly feud? Who can I talk to about the very depths of my spirit and what eats away at me, because time is moving so fast and I'm not fulfilling my purpose? When my time comes to pass on from this realm and I'm taking my last breath, will I be content or will I have nothing to show for my life here? What will my legacy be? How do I heal the Earth's waters and bring back the tigers from the brink of extinction? Should I foster children, or take in refugees or homeless women? Why does my neighbour cut down our precious, bird-sheltering trees as soon as growth appears after a harsh winter? How can I quieten my mind and lay down this heavy case full of the world's problems that I carry around every day?* All this before 7 a.m!

The radio was playing Rick Astley on a 1980s classics hour and, in between distractions, I sat out on the porch on a small pouffe that had absorbed more tears and cigarette ash than any inanimate object should have to, propping up my sighs and despair. *How do I get out of here? Does no one hear my heart? Does no one in this world think like me? Of course they don't, you fool,* I thought. Then, I continued to sip my tea and scroll through my phone, past adverts for dog nappies and pictures of what my sister had for tea the night before.

My heart fell through my stomach, tears again rolled down my face. *Is this it?* I agonized... *this can't just be it.* Arms outstretched and head to the sky in a weak but desperate voice, I called to the universe, 'Please help me!'

Then I stopped scrolling, as a video appeared on my feed of a First Nations man and woman speaking from behind a wooden desk out in the yard, with a run-down garage as the backdrop and huge pine trees billowing and swaying above. It looked warm – definitely not England. They were preparing to speak and it appeared they were serious. The man continued to settle himself and began drumming and singing. He then spoke in his native language and, although I couldn't understand his words, I could feel his energy and intent. Somehow connecting across the cosmos, I felt he was looking directly at me. I was mesmerized; I fell into a trance-like state and for the next three hours I did not move from that tatty old pouffe. I listened to someone speak in ways my spirit recognized. My heart filled with every sentence he spoke.

Beside him sat a beautiful woman with olive skin, piercing brown eyes and hair that rivalled Rapunzel's, braided and laid to one side across her shoulder. The man had dark hair to his shoulders, slightly receding, and he wore a traditional top in bright colours of blue and red. He talked of honouring our grandmothers, and how the women (life-givers) were sacred and revered in their culture before colonization came to infect their shores. They both spoke of the moon and how crucial she was to life on Earth but that she was under threat from the corporations of the industrial world.

The man and woman were part of a small group, who went live on social media every week to expose these threats as well as the continued genocide and oppression of their peoples. They spoke of the importance of ceremony in so many forms: the ceremony of the strawberries, the solstice, the waters. They had a ceremony for everything and, before any words were spoken, they gave thanks in their native tongue, called the Ohenton Karhiwatekwen ('the words before all else'). The words were then translated into Canadian French and English by the woman with long braided hair. She was from the Zapotec nation in South America; her name was Edith.

So, this group, this handful of people, were also trying to unravel the conditioning of the forcibly imposed western patriarchal control over their society. They spoke of returning our 'mothers back to power and their natural seat of authority'. What!? You mean there are nations in this world who were led by women peacefully for thousands of years before religion invaded the minds of men? I had never heard such words spoken about women in public. My mind was blown and, from that moment on, I was determined to be a part of this work they were doing; to be part of the life they believed in and that I'd longed for since my eyes could see, and I felt a calling deep in my blood.

And so, from my little council estate house in a quiet English town to their longhouse in a place called Kahnawake, a 'reserve' for the Mohawk peoples of Canada, I was about to embark on the quest of my lifetime, 5,111km (3,176 miles) away, across the great waters of the Atlantic.

Visions

Early the next morning as I woke, I was filled with energy and hope. I immediately gave thanks and continued into a vision or daydream as I began to meditate on what had happened, setting intentions with the power of the new moon.

I shall try to describe what I saw. From my mouth, I blew words across the land that spread in whispers, like great waves or an invisible boom that you can feel but barely see. From my third eye, in the middle of my forehead, I threw out seeds that would fall at every woman's feet. From that, she will 'know what is to be done'. She will plant that seed and nurture it and help it grow like our daughters. The seed was corn, and it grew tall and straight, pulled skywards by Grandmother Moon.

As my outstretched arms came back, my hands cupped together, holding a ball of fire that was thrown out across the land, and every woman who touched it was set on fire, though not in a hurtful way, as they were protected from any damage. They stood tall with the fire in their hands, like beacons shining across the land as a warning and symbol to others that they are the light and that change is coming. The women shall be beacons of light and peace to spread this message.

The fire then continued past the people and across the Earth, purifying and cleansing, until it came to the shores. Instead of being extinguished by the sea, it remained alight as it plunged down into the deep oceans and cleansed our seas until it reached the very core of the Earth.

Finally, as I stood and released my arms out wide, feathers shot out from the sides of each arm and turned into great birds, possibly eagles, to carry those spreading the message; to provide protection and shelter.

Two weeks before this vision, I had two others concerning women rising and our connection with Mother Earth. I am not saying this dream or vision is about me. It is about women in general and how I imagine Mother Earth herself.

Through most of my life, I have thought and lived internally with a heart that loved the land and nature. Everything these native people represented resonated with me. Their connection with the land and love of Mother Earth are things that had always sparked something deep in me and influenced everything I did, wrote, listened to and wore. I know my family struggled with this, never really understanding where it came from, and so I lived it out alone, almost in silence, for many years. I know that every day of my life, I dreamed of having contact with these peoples, living ceremonially and traditionally, and also having the chance to stand up and start to right the wrongs inflicted on them by our nations.

Destiny

My heart manifested the greatest interaction I could have wished for when I met Stuart Myiow and Wahiakeron of the Kanienkeha'ka territory, as well the most amazing group of women working alongside them in the longhouse. Their intention was to enact the Great Law of Peace in our lives, and to be a beacon for others to see that there is hope and a place where we can collectively work towards saving our Mother Earth and moon.

We all have a destiny and purpose, but figuring out what it may be is one of life's great mysteries. By following our intuition, the sense in our gut and dreams in our minds, we each can carve out a path that brings unimaginable joy and wisdom, that no amount of academic study or psychedelics can bring.

I live on this Earth to walk the path of the medicine women of my ancestry and learn from today's abundant and rich tapestry of cultures from all over the world. Only five weeks after the vision, I flew to Canada – part of what was once called Turtle Island, before it was split and renamed as Canada and the United States of America and colonized by the British and other invaders. I journeyed there, to the longhouse of the Kanienkeha'ka peoples, in the hope of attempting to bring healing from my line, from the atrocities caused and hundreds of years of oppression and genocide inflicted upon the First Nation people. It was an attempt to build bridges to their peaceful culture and to join a nation of women who have risen from the Earth bound by our feminine law to restore healing and peace to our chaotic, war ridden, disconnected world.

The Journey

I arrived in Canada for the first time on 23 August 2019, carrying a suitcase with enough clothes, Yorkshire tea and camping supplies to last me three weeks (when I say the Yorkshire tea took up more room in the suitcase than my clothes, I might not be exaggerating). I also brought another larger case holding something I had been working on in secret. The case held a story of the time I turned a 45kg (100lb) mound of bison into leather that would go on to live in the rightful hands of the nation of Kanienkeha'ka people.

I embarked on the journey through the pine forests of Ontario towards Montreal and across the bridge to Kahnawake in a car I've never driven, through a country I've never driven through, with strange signs, and to a place I've never been to, or knew how to find.

Despite the challenges before me, I was so eager to get on the road. I had spent my first night in Canada with my friend Lisa who had kindly collected me from the airport and took me back to her smallholding where my gorgeous boy Blu was living with her other dogs and horses. Blu was one of Kes's 12 pups. Lisa had wanted some of Kes's bloodline so much that she flew across from Canada when Blu was three months old to collect him. I thought if someone is willing to make that sort of sacrifice for my pup, he's surely going to a good home. If she hadn't come for Blu, I would have kept him as one of my own. He's such an adorable little dog with big blue eyes – hence the name. Little did I know that a year later, I'd be seeing him again in his home in Canada! Lisa lived just a few hours from the longhouse and she kindly lent me her car for the duration of my visit so I could make my way across the country.

So many synchronicities happened on the journey, and everything had been written in the stars long before I was born. The road was long, a vast expanse in front of me lined each side by huge, towering white pines. This tree represents the six nations confederacy, or the Haudenosaunee, consisting of the Mohawk, Oneida, Onedage, Kuyuga, Seneca and Tuscarora peoples.

I live on this earth to walk the path of the medicine women of my ancestry and learn from today's abundant and rich tapestry of cultures from all over the world.

The white pine is the tree of life native to these lands for thousands of years and holds much wisdom and medicine. If you become sick in winter, collect the solid, amber-coloured sap that oozes from her bark through summer and suck on small pieces, and your illness will disappear within hours. The buds also give off a pungent taste when chewed. This has a similar effect to pine resin and will halt the onset of any cold or flu. Much like the medicine of the cedar tree, the leaves can be steeped in boiling water and infused to make a tonic that will soothe any winter ailments caused by the cold virus.

This knowledge, among a vast library of wisdom, was freely given to European sailors who began to arrive in the Americas from 1492 onwards. These men didn't know the terrain, plants or food sources in the region. Tired and sick from weeks of travelling, they would surely have died had the indigenous people not offered out their hands in grace and kindness to help their fellow beings who were looking for refuge. Little did they know this act of kindness would be the end of their ancient, relatively peaceful way of life.

The Two Row Wampum Treaty

After the first European settlers arrived, a treaty was made between them and the Indigenous Haudenosaunee people: the Two Row Wampum Treaty. ('Wampum' means 'clause'.) This treaty is everlasting and still enacted in the justice system of the US and Canada to this day. The treaty stated that the native people would welcome the settlers, but they must 'paddle their own canoe'. It acknowledged that both were travelling along the same river, but that they would not interfere with each other's culture or heritage. If either needed the other nation's help, they may call on them. The Two Row Wampum Treaty was agreed and signed, and a belt was made to honour it. This belt symbolizes the agreement and conditions under which the Haudenosaunee welcomed the newcomers to this land. It is a long narrow ceremonial piece around 60cm (2ft) long and 25cm (10in) wide. The belt is white, which represents the white water of the rapids, with two brown stripes, representing the two canoes belonging to each side, Native American and European.

A section of this 1613 agreement between the Haudenosaunee people and representatives of the Dutch government declares:

You say that you are our father and I am your son.

We say, 'We will not be like Father and Son, but like Brothers'.

This wampum belt confirms our words. These two rows will symbolize two paths or two vessels, traveling down the same river together. One, a birch bark canoe, will be for the Indian People, their laws, their customs and their ways. We shall each travel the river together, side by side, but in our own boat. Neither of us will make compulsory laws or interfere in the internal affairs of the other. Neither of us will try to steer the other's vessel.

However, soon after that agreement was made, the British, Dutch and other settlers broke this treaty and took advantage of the First Nations, taking their lands, women, animals and children and slaughtering them. They raped their sacred land and culture. Men, drunk on gluttony and ambition, tore through village after village, burning them to the ground, raping, killing or taking the women as slaves and pillaging hides, food and winter supplies.

These men came from Europe, a continent filled with a sickness that was carried to the lands of the Turtle and spread like a wildfire bush of sun-beaten prairie grass ignited by the hot July sun. This wildfire showed no mercy, it was soulless and senseless and took no prisoners.

The white man's coming was foretold for decades before he arrived. It is said that these stories were based on the arrival of the Vikings to (so-called) Newfoundland several centuries earlier. For in the years that followed, as the European settlers and Indigenous peoples began to live among each other more, stories of strange man-beasts invading their shores hundreds of years earlier began to circulate. For political reasons, and the ingrained arrogance of Europeans, many of these stories were rejected and never even mentioned again in history books – at least until these past few decades.

Wahiakeron, an elder of the Kanienkeha'ka people and Wolf Clan, told me that he believed that initially there was fighting between the Vikings and Indigenous peoples. It was the first time they had seen men with beards. Facial hair was not normal on Turtle Island, so they saw the Europeans as a separate animal and felt threatened by them. But they resolved their differences and the Vikings settled all along the Eastern seaboard. They established homes built into the land underground and respected the local way of life much more than later European settlers. More conflict did ensue eventually, and the Vikings retreated back to Greenland and Iceland by the 13th century due to the harsh weather and fear of the native tribes. However, a few remained and mixed with the Indigenous people leaving obvious physical characteristics, including blue eyes, red hair and fair skin!

First Meeting

As I neared the reserve of Kahnawake, passing over the St Lawrence River on the south shore, Montreal disappearing behind me into the distance, I felt my stomach turn and my eyes started to fill with tears. This happens when I go to a place of historical importance, not just in world history, but soul history – a place that I feel I'm returning to, though I've never been there before. The history is tangible, I can taste it! I, we, have the capacity to sense a previous lifetime and summon it into our bones – it's deep.

Clinging onto the steering wheel as I negotiated strange motorway passes and slip roads, I kept one eye fixed on the road, and the other on the navigation system and the other (that'll be my internal third eye) on the path of history I was now entering. This place looked nothing like it did 500 years ago. The river was polluted, and the trees were choked with toxic fumes from the cascade of cars that filed past like rats on a wheel, stuck in a never-ending cycle of work, eat, sleep, repeat. In my mind's eye, I imagined a place before the sky was filled with metal and brick, a place straight out of the books and films that I'd sat and watched with my father. Even at such a young age, I knew of the genocide in this region and would weep inside for what was done to its people and the picture that was painted of them. That little girl rode with me then, in the seat next to me in the car, looking out of the window into a new world riddled with disease and disconnected from the vibrant beautiful peaceful homes that existed here along the wide river below the bridge.

I pulled into the yard where the longhouse stood. I immediately recognized the trees billowing above the building and the flags on the wooden shed that had been my focus every Wednesday night on Zoom for the last few weeks. I was nervous to finally meet the people I had connected with so deeply, but I was also like an excited little child, ready to face what lay in store for the next three weeks of my stay here.

The door opened to the wooden longhouse and out strode a giant of a man – Stuart Myiow. He was quiet and stern faced, but he came to me and enveloped me in an embrace that spoke a thousand words. A tall man with golden-brown skin and black shoulder-length hair swept back, he was handsome and mesmerizing. He was powerful and bold and oozed arrogance. He knew he was a beautiful man externally, but I wanted to know if he lived true to the words he continually proclaimed. Was he the life-protector he swore he was, holding women and their power in reverence? Or was he the same as the men I knew back home who thought only with their ego and not their integrity. 'Follow me', he said. At this point, I was so taken aback at the size of the man I forgot to speak. The woman with the black, Rapunzel-like hair, Edith, asked if I was okay and with a crackly voice and a beaming smile I replied: 'Yes, where are we going?' She stayed silent and led me down a path into the grounds behind the longhouse, where the gardens were full of corn growing tall and bright green.

Set in about an acre of land were tall trees sheltering the green, freshly cut lawn that held space for the tepee at the far end of the garden. A few tents were scattered between wooden structures and rows of trees and beyond, out of sight, was the ceremonial Three Sisters Garden. The corn here had been planted in circular rows, leading into the centre where a tall wooden shell of a tepee stood. I walked up the path to the tepee, which was lined with fire lanterns, and inside it stood Stuart, Edith and another man (who I recognized from some of our online sessions). Wahiakeron was his name and he was whittling a small wooden pipe from a freshly cut pine branch. He looked up at me and smiled. His eyes the brightest blue, like a tropical ocean, piercing but gentle. His hair was grey and hung around his shoulders. I knew nothing of him but immediately I was drawn to his spirit and handsome stature. I knew he was a strong character without even saying a word. His smile settled me and, as Stuart began speaking, I realized they were performing a ceremony for me. It was to welcome me, the first English woman to come to their longhouse with a good heart, mind and intention in 500 years, as I was told!

A Ceremonial Welcome

The ceremony was a re-enactment of the time the Two Row Wampum Treaty was first created and the wampum belt handed over to the Europeans in the 17th century, except this time it would be placed in the hands of a woman, a British woman. Stuart Myiow, of the Wolf Clan of the Kanienkeha'ka, declared that the Two Row Wampum Treaty will now be placed in the hands of a woman from England.

I was handed an eagle feather, which belonged to Stuart's recently passed father, along with dried corn (sacred to the native peoples as a food source and medicine), and finally the Two Row Wampum Treaty belt that had been used in their family for many generations.

Several women had gathered at the longhouse in Kahnawake, as part of a newly formed women's nation movement, relearning the old ways of the people. They performed a recital of the Great Law of Peace. Over the course of the next three weeks, we would learn together, eat and bond together on a subject so precious and ancient I knew I was witnessing a very rare event. The Great Law of Peace is known to so few people, yet it affects so many. There is always a reason why certain knowledge is kept hidden away and quiet: because it is so powerful.

The three weeks I spent at the longhouse in Kahnawake changed my life. I met the most wonderful people, who I will be connected with for the rest of my life. They performed a leaving ceremony for me the night before I went, and I have never felt such love in one space as I did that night as they sent the feather around the circle and told me their thoughts about me and my purpose. I declared that I would work hard and have done so every day since to correct our true relationship with the Indigenous peoples in accordance with the Two Row Wampum Peace Treaty.

The Great Law of Peace

'Grand council of the six united nations under the Great Law of Peace is a derivative of the Law of Creation on which all life is formed.'
Wahiakeron

It is said that the inspirational, ancient Iroquois Great Law of Peace planted the seeds that went on to form the representative democracy of the United States of America, which stands to this day.

The Iroquois Confederacy was founded by Dekanawida, known as the Peacemaker, and is unquestionably the oldest democracy still in existence on the planet. The Iroquois Confederacy, also known as the six nations, refer to themselves as the Haudenosaunee (pronounced, *hoo-dee-noh-SHAW-nee*), meaning 'peoples of the longhouse'. This refers to their long bark-covered longhouses that sheltered many families and formed the spaces for communal ceremonies.

The longhouses in an Iroquois Confederacy village

The Iroquois Confederacy model of governance is based on the seventh generation to come. This principle dictates that decisions made today should be sustainable for seven generations into the future. Their democratic principles focus strongly on the creation and importance of kinship bonds that promote leadership in which honour is not earned by material gain, but by service to others.

The Iroquois, or Haudenosaunee Confederacy, has been in place since time immemorial. According to their teachings, the Creator sent Dekanawida to spread the 'kariwiio' or good mind. Aiionwatha, commonly known as Hiawatha, helped the Peacemaker teach the laws of peace to the Haudenosaunee. They travelled from community to community, urging the chiefs of each nation to agree to the Great Law of Peace and succeeded in founding the only government with a direct connection to the Creator.

The Great Law of Peace is a complex yet well implemented historical method of holding negotiations to restore peace in times of conflict or war. The clan mothers were the authority and the decision-makers. The law is long and thorough, and the methodology has worked for thousands of years. Those who still know and honour the law uphold it in their culture throughout Turtle Island. I believe, from what I've learned through the recital of the law and during my time in the company of the people who teach it, that we could all benefit and learn so much from this successful ancient law. It peacefully resolves disputes in times of uncertainty and turmoil.

The symbol of the Great Law of Peace is the Great White Pine, with roots outstretched from north to south, east to west, and any nation choosing to follow the law would be welcomed beneath the shade of the tree. Within each nation were many different chiefs and clans, and each clan was named after animals significant to its culture, from wolf to turtle, bear to hawk, heron to deer. Above the image of the tree was an eagle that could see far away and alert the confederacy of approaching enemies. Each law that makes up the Great Law is represented by a wampum belt, declaring the rules of that specific law. Originally, five nations sealed the Great Law by tying together a single arrow from each nation, to symbolize their bonding. There are now six nations.

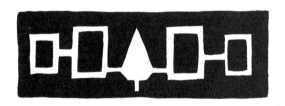

A wampum with a symbol of the Great Law of Peace, showing a white pine in the centre

With his mission fulfilled, Dekanawida vanished, promising that if the Great Law of Peace should fail, the people were to call his name in the trees and bushes and he would return.

This is an example of one of the wampums, or clauses, in the Great Law of Peace, translated by Wahiakeron:

Wampum 6: Dekanawida Appoints the Mohawk Chiefs Leaders of the Confederacy

tekanakwita wakherihonten mohawka akontihenteseke wisk natekahontsaneren otiohkwa. mohawks ononhkwa kanonhsesne ne kowanen skennen tanon enierhiwaiake tekaianerahseraneren a'ontohetste tsitkatsenhaien katiohkwakon sontohetste mohawks wahonwatorhiwaiakse.

iah tsikatsenhaien kaianerahsera tha'onton tsik mohawks ienhonneseke.

I, Dekanawida, appoint the Mohawk statesmen the head and the leaders of the Five Nations League. The Mohawk statesmen are the foundation of the Great Peace and it shall therefore be against the Great Binding Law to pass measures in the Council of the League after the Mohawk statesmen have protested against them.

No Council of the League shall be legal unless all of the statesmen of the Mohawks are present.

The first time I heard of this ancient constitution was through the longhouse online teachings that I watched from England in the early hours of the morning. Afterwards, I'd wait for the sun to come up and then go back to bed for an hour before starting my day.

The law was originally verbal, but a written document was created by a colonizer who was ruled by his own religion. The First Nations society extends back at least 2,000 years and much of it was originally matrilineal. The grandmothers held authority and they sought to bring peace between warring tribes to save their sons who were dying in battle. As Wahiakeron told me: 'Of course, peace was established by the women. As a mother, you want only peace for your child. Men seek to settle scores through war and violence.' He said that his mother stopped him from going to war in Vietnam: 'I did not raise you to go and kill other people on their own land. We do not know them; unless they invade us here you must stay away.'

Later, as society changed and men did not want a woman to be the heroine of the story for a significant law like this, they raised up a male hero, Aiionwatha or Hiawatha. He was praised for gathering the nations together alongside the Dekanawida.

The more I learned about the power of the women in his nation, the more I felt a deep surge of passion in my belly and, one day before I arrived on Turtle Island, I walked up to the hill near my workshop on an impulse. Looking out over the River Trent below, I found an old hawthorn tree and began to engrave a symbol of peace into her bark. I took a picture of the carving and sat down on a fallen log next to it while I sparked up a cigarette and drank my flask of tea.

These words flowed out of my mouth and onto the page:

> *The Great Law of Peace, the oldest constitution in existence, now engraved and rooted in the land so as the scars heal upon this tree, they will begin to also heal our Mother Earth from the wars, corruption and destruction that has plagued our shores*

and those nations we have invaded and persecuted across the great waters since we lost our souls and community to a patriarchal society and destroyed our true love and connection to our home.

If you listen, on a quiet day, you can hear her breathing, her heart beating....

I sent my words and the photo across to Canada. Then, later that evening, a YouTube video of their latest class appeared, talking about me and what I had done.

Apparently, Stuart was astonished! On the video, he relayed a dream he had the night before I sent the carved image. In his dream, his face was covered in tears of joy and happiness and, as he pointed to the image above on a screen, he says it is because I had carved out the Dekanawida to come out from the trees on this side of the world.

He paced back and forth in the longhouse around a long wooden table, surrounded by men and women of different ages. Wahiakeron, the language keeper, sat at the top of the table with Stuart. His presence was animated on the subject and he continued, 'to have her bring forward, even cry out for the Great Law of Peace. To call out Dekanawida's name and they are doing it without even knowing it, carving his face in the trees for him to come out. That's like they carved a portal for him to come through on that side [in England].' He was referring to the fact that, without knowing, I had fulfilled a prophecy within their Great Law.

Dekanawida went across the great waters after he completed his mission on Turtle Island, saying that if he was ever needed again, the people were to call his name in the trees and he would return. I had called out his name by carving the symbol into the tree. I opened the portal for him to restore peace across the great waters.

It felt surreal for me to hear these words, having had no idea of the story at the time when I instinctively carved the image. On the video, Stuart sat down and turned to point at the screen again, 'How did she know? She did not know that Dekanawida said he was going to the trees to cover himself in bark and if you ever need me again you go to the woods and call out my name... You see the moment we enact the Two Row Wampum into the proper place, things start to happen. It's like plugging the power back in!'

His closing statement was 'and now we know what to expect!'

Also, I was unaware that I had carved this symbol on the day of the dead in the Mayan calendar. The day translates as 'renewal', or in Kanienkeha'ka language, '*Ah un away du say*', meaning 'the regeneration of a person'. Wahiakeron said this was happening to me – a death of the old and a rebirth into the new – and it was also affecting my son, even though as yet he knew nothing of my connection with the longhouse. But the mind is a powerful tool and can be felt in mysterious ways, even transcending oceans.

CHAPTER 15

The Spirit of the Buffalo

B uffalo, also known as bison, are spiritually powerful animals for the tribes of Turtle Island. The Indigenous peoples of the Great Plains perform many rituals, dances and prayers to honour the dangerous but life-sustaining art of buffalo hunting. In many myths, buffalo have brought themselves to humans as their food source and medicine, so are deeply respected and honoured. Like all large herd animals, buffalo graze and move across the landscape and this is what has kept their precious habitats finely tuned, balanced and thriving for thousands of years. Wahiakeron told me that many of the harmful atmospheric changes on our planet occurred when the relationship between the buffalo and the people who cared for them for centuries broke down. These people knew the vital role the buffalo played in keeping the earth and the atmosphere healthy; the animals locked huge quantities of carbon into the soil as they migrated and fertilized the grasslands in a perfectly symbiotic cycle of seed, sprout, spread, swallow and so on.

Buffalo might have sealed their own fate, however. As the huge herds thundered across the landscape, they kicked up enormous dust clouds into the atmosphere, which were carried across the great waters of the Atlantic and deposited in Britain and the rest of Europe. This is how the aristocrats and royalty of Britain knew there were distant lands to be discovered and, upon invasion, the first thing the European settlers did was to cut that communication between the First Nations people and the buffalo, explains Stuart Myiow of the Kanienkeha'ka nation.

The population of buffalo plummeted during the height of European colonization; an estimated 30 million animals were reduced to a few hundred by the end of the 19th century. One way to kill a people is to kill their most valuable food source. But the buffalo is not just a food source, she is also the spirit of a land, a people, a nation.

The slaughter of the buffalo was seen as a way to starve the First Nations people into submission and make them reliant on the colonial government, but buffalo-hunting also became a big part of the economy for the white settlers. In 1873, an economic depression hit and thousands of 'buffalo runners' tore through the herds, killing around 50 at a time. Their hides, along with their tongues and humps (used in medicine) were taken and the rest of the buffalos' bodies were left to rot where they lay across the prairies. The vast open prairies, once teeming with life, became buffalo graveyards, filling the air with death and decay. It was documented that skins piled up as high as houses, so the markets became flooded, and the price of hides dropped. Despite this, hunting increased. This was an undeniably barbaric chapter in human history and it is difficult to comprehend the grief caused by the loss of such a peaceful animal and the culture it supported. Fortunately, the buffalo held on, and now their numbers have risen to around 25,000.

I knew within a matter of days of contact with the longhouse what my mission was.

There are no coincidences in life. When I began searching for a place to obtain a buffalo hide in England, of course there just happened to be a bison farm down the road, 20 minutes from my house! Not something you'd think likely, right? The farmer also just 'happened' to have a hide in the freezer, which I bought from her for £100! 'What will you do with that?' asked the lady who owned the farm. 'Well, I'm going to tan it and make it into a leather robe, then take it across to Canada as a gift, to apologize for raping the native First Nations of their precious source of buffalo and pushing both the Indigenous people and native animals to the brink of extinction by the men of this country.' She looked at me wide-eyed, with a look of startled uneasiness, and bid me on my way. I smirked knowing that I'd lit a spark of intrigue in her. And there began five weeks of toil and tantrums to turn this 45-kg (100-lb) lump of flesh into a beautiful, soft buffalo hide and somehow get it through customs and into the rightful hands of the Kanienkeha'ka people of the longhouse in Canada.

Preparing the Buffalo Hide

There are many fantastic, advanced technologies today for making leather, but I'm a stubborn witch and wanted to do this as authentically as possible. I wanted to really FEEL the process of revival within the spirit of this hide, walking in the footsteps of the ancients who did this ritually and in ceremonies with absolute gratitude and reverence.

So, I set about making a bone tool that would be similar to the instrument used to prepare hides before metal scrapers. The bone was a cattle femur with the bottom edge cut diagonally and serrated to give good purchase when pounding away at the flesh to remove it from the membrane. This pounding process took nine hours of work, with no time to stop, because I was working against the clock to get the hide on a frame and allow it time to dry. The fur falls out rapidly when wet and I needed to work quickly with this defrosted hide. There was no point in making a patchy piece of leather. A buffalo's full winter coat is a spectacle of grandeur and I needed to salvage it.

My wooden frames were too small for a huge, heavy buffalo hide, but Harry's trampoline could work.... Many bribery attempts later, I removed the cover from the trampoline and began stringing up the hide. It was the most genius idea I'd had in a long while. It worked perfectly, because it was round, so I could roll it around with ease, put it on the legs and cover it with tarpaulin to be smoked. At the beginning of this process and throughout, I began by burning herbs and speaking with my ancestors and the moon to help me complete this task.

I had never embarked on such an undertaking before, and the ride wasn't smooth. I almost lost the fur at a few stages; it began to fall out, so I raced to get heat and fans on the deteriorating areas. I was in contact with a good friend in America for advice and discovered that washing-up liquid would halt the progression of bacteria that could ruin the edges. It was an absolute emotional rollercoaster. I also took the hide to a farmer friend to power-hose some of the dirt and flesh off, and mistakenly blasted a hole in it, but that didn't stop me. I ploughed on.

To begin with the stench was foul; the smell of bubbling sheep brains on my camping stove was terrible, but combined with soap, butter and oil this softened the hide. I scraped, stretched, bounced, danced, cried, bled, dug deep and grafted. All along, every moment I felt I was being watched. Not because I was filming the whole process, but because I could see a circle of elders holding me up. Women with long braided hair, with painted bodies, cracked skin and deeply scarred faces smiling, cheering me on, willing me to not give up.

I'm not sure how many women have recently tanned a huge buffalo hide single-handedly in England, although I know this used to happen many years ago. I worked with such heart and intention that I know it will be a memory carved in my mind (and back!) for forever. Hides like this are meant to be made in a community – in a tribe, a gathering – with everyone sharing the toil and working in unison to create an heirloom that will last for decades. I hope the next time I tan a buffalo hide, it will be with a group of women 'waulking' – a Gaelic term meaning to work together with wool. We will be singing and crafting together to rebuild not only the connections needed so desperately in today's world, but for the spirits that are reborn from such a powerful beast and sent out into the world.

So, I worked in secret on something that was maybe written in the stars and placed along my life path many years ago. It was not only my most challenging, humbling piece of work to date but, apart from the birth of my son, the greatest accomplishment of my life – not just physically, but in terms of what it represented.

The hide was to be presented to the longhouse as a gift and small token of reparation. It was an apology and an act of healing for the genocide of Indigenous people and their life source, the buffalo, by the people of my home country. To tan a hide is to bring rebirth and restoration. I engraved the symbol of the Great Law of Peace into the leather and set off for Turtle Island.

So, here, I will honour my female line, as I know there were strong formidable women in my past, women who saw beyond the norm, women who wouldn't be silenced. All women of my line had a hand in this, and I honour them through this act of healing.

How did you get that through customs, you ask? Well... with help from the 'Bison Gods'. I disguised it, held my breath, didn't declare it and smiled sweetly at the security guard as I waltzed past casually. It's not illegal to take hide into the country, but I didn't want to risk the authorities seizing it if they found a tiny speck of dirt on it, or found out it wasn't chemically tanned. That would not only have been the end of all that effort, but a whole lineage of hope that took several generations to muster, all gone on an airport conveyor.

The Gift

I had been at the longhouse for two days and we had begun the recital of the Great Law of Peace, which would take three weeks. This is when I presented the buffalo skin I had been hiding in my tent since my arrival. I spoke out to everyone gathered for the ceremony, although I was terrified about whether they'd accept or like it. I pulled back a blanket cover to reveal the huge 2m- (6ft-) wide hide, with fluffy chestnut-brown fur, thick and long at the neck, short and dense across the body.

There was silence for a few seconds, which felt like an eternity, until Stuart pronounced his amazement and surprise at what lay on the floor beneath them. Everyone came to gather, to touch and smell the hide, and hug me. I can't describe the feeling of relief that washed over me. The anticipation of their reaction had been so intense. I smiled and left the scene briefly to go and bawl my eyes out in my tent. The feeling of relief from such an undertaking, one that was so important to me, came flooding out and seeped down into the grass beneath me. It is done. Healing had begun from my line and my nation.

The start of transformation in my life began in 2019. In that year, I lost my father, my marriage ended, my sheep flock was sold, my son left home, and my 14-year-old dog and my nine-year-old cat both died. Grief comes in many forms… but we carry on because it's part of life; life is pain but it's also love, and we must remember we bring life into this world as much as we endure death.

Despite this, it was one of the best years of my life in other ways. Through suffering and death, I found *life*. Not only was the buffalo reborn in my tired sore hands, but I followed the call of my heart. In doing so, I shed many layers of conditioning and patriarchal chains, and through working the hide I was also reborn. I saw who I was, and why I was here. I am not the same woman since I carved that bone tool and met the flesh of the sacred beast.

There was much hope in the hide, it had much to absorb. The buffalo spirit was reinstated and my spirit will live on in it. The greatest gift I could leave – my footprint on the Earth, the intention and purpose it inspires – was there, in that hide, worked by my hands and heart.

Vision Quest

Does anything I've shared here make you wonder how I got here? How did I know what to ask for, pursue, dream? Finding one's purpose or next step in life can be overwhelming, consuming and demoralizing – never knowing where to start, how to find your calling of how to answer questions that invade your overloaded brain like *Who am I?* or *Why am I here?*

Well, there is something you can do if you feel called to; it's called a vision quest or rite of passage. Many of you may have been through these experiences and journeyed through quests without even knowing that's what you were doing. Yet, they can be intentionally explored and this practice, or change, has been carried out in Indigenous American cultures for centuries. The Celts and other tribal cultures also illustrate and tell of a deep transformational time – of a passage. The reasons for this passage are unique to the individual and can be very different for each of us. They can include birth or death – real and symbolic – career changes, marriage, divorce, menopause and other major life events.

You may have felt acutely aware of the increasingly hectic times in which we live, and experience an urge to connect with ourselves and nature more than ever before. Such quests can be deeply empowering, cathartic and enlightening, and strengthen your resolve. These quests plug you back in with the spirit and creative force within all of us, helping us to seek the answers we are searching for, and to discover what really matters, our purpose and what we want out of life.

The power comes by handing over control of these questions to Mother Nature, the spirit and your inner self.

These initiations are a kind of rebirth; they can be truly life changing. If you approach them with an open yearning heart, you will be welcomed, tested, revealed, shattered, ripped apart, put back together, and built up again, piece by piece. Like unpeeling the layers of an onion, the quest may reveal you at your core. It may reveal the young girl or boy who was there at your birth, but over years of conditioning, abuse, trauma, lack of acceptance, has had their beautiful light covered with many masks. Nature has a way of unearthing your soul. Be prepared: it may not be easy but it's absolutely necessary, because the world needs you and you owe it to yourself and those of your lineage.

The journey helps you to become more mindful and aware of everything in existence, and realize that you are part of something greater than yourself and your surroundings.

You will emerge energized, cleansed and passionate about what lies ahead. You may experience visions, an epiphany or enlightenment. In essence, you will find meaning and truth in your life – it is a symbolic awakening.

This quest can be made to suit your lifestyle and time constraints. There are no rules other than discipline and earnestly seeking the wisdom from the universe for your life and circumstances.

MAKING YOUR QUEST

Take yourself out of your daily life and travel out into nature. Camp or find a place that feels safe. Three days away is recommended, but a full day is still valuable and can bring as much wisdom – although a longer period obviously offers the body more opportunity to settle into a state of awareness.

Create a circle around where you stay and try to stay within it. But again, if you are not staying overnight be mindful of your area in the day. Stay with a tree and sit below it, leaning into the bark and sheltering below the boughs.

Fasting is recommended – not only does an empty stomach help to declutter the mind, but there are also myriad physical benefits of an extended overnight fast. I find it empties the stomach and therefore the mind of clutter. I suggest avoiding sugar for the week leading up to this time, which will help to prepare your body for fasting and reduce unsettling hunger pangs. The point of fasting is to strip away any distractions that comfort food brings. It makes me feel exposed and vulnerable, and forces me to listen to what my body is saying to me. It is essential, though, to stay hydrated.

Boredom and distractions will come to unsettle you, but, like hunger, they will pass. Try to avoid noticing the time, it will only make it pass more slowly and draw your attention away from the real reason for being there. Light a fire or candle, burn herbs such as mugwort, which works in the dream world to bring your visions to life. Do light exercise and meditation, closing your eyes and seeing what appears. If you go out on the full moon, which I highly recommend, then stare at her for as long as you can.

When I did this, the moon started to turn blue around her perimeter and then sacred geometrical patterns covered her surface. Within the deep belly of the moon, I saw a ball of white fire circling and, as I eventually closed my eyes, I saw my third eye surrounded by a triangular shape and bright purple colours fading to blue and pink. I promise I wasn't intoxicated!

Pray and ask for guidance, always giving thanks for the beauty surrounding you, your beating heart and the breath in your lungs. Declare your life and heart to the sun as she sets and blow out your words to be caught on the wind.

When you return home and the days pass, recall all you encountered during your time in nature, re-emerging again by journaling and keeping a record of the life-changing time you spend alone with the Mother. You should always treat the process with reverence and honour those from whom the rite of passage and quest originate.

CHAPTER 16

Wolf Clan

In recognition of tanning the buffalo hide, Wahiakeron adopted me into his family and gave me a name. This is the name nature knows me by: I am Iekawehatie ('she paddles along'), adopted into the Wolf Clan ('Hung about the neck' – which means my mother was not native) of the Kanienkeha'ka (Mohawk) people. The wolf is the Okwaho, the path-maker.

Wahiakeron performed a naming ceremony in line with longhouse protocol; he showed me to the Creator and asked her to accept me under her protection. I stood in traditional clothes given to me for the occasion, as Wahiakeron spoke out in his native language, Kanienkeha'ka: 'I present Iekawehatie, we do not know what she brings to us, maybe she is a hunter? Maybe she is a teacher.... If she is sick, bring her the medicines she needs to heal.' We paced from one end of the longhouse to the other, from where the sun rises to where the sun sets. Wahiakeron gave me a necklace that had been gifted to him by the Mayan people. He burned tobacco and sage and sent the offerings into the smoke to be sealed by Mother Earth, eldest brother, the Sun, and Grandmother Moon. This was a moment in time that eclipsed all others, as though everything was leading to this day. I was swept along as though being tossed on the rapids without oars, free to go where the wind and waves took me. My eight-year-old self would have been so proud of me.

Wahiakeron became such a positive part of my experience there in that land; we made such a close bond and we are now forever entwined. On my return back home, I took on the role of being the Two Row Wampum liaison here in Britain, beaming their sacred moon teachings via video into universities and schools. This is such a great honour for me, and the seed planted in these minds will grow and live long in the memory of those who hear the teachings.

CHAPTER 17

Moon

Every night, no matter what stage the moon is in, I look at it in wonder. The moon saved my life.

According to the Indigenous nations of the world who embrace the moon as their grandmother and guide, the dark or new moon is the feminine moon and the full moon is the masculine. Celtic mythology also sees darkness as representing the sacred feminine. It was when I was at my lowest point, that rock-bottom stage, that I discovered the mysterious and comforting power of the moon.

After my marriage died, I finally gathered the strength to break free from my tormented heart and spirit and was able to let it all go. I am amazed at how easy it is to write about this, yet, in reality, letting go took a huge amount of strength and wisdom, and many years of intense work. After living with deep psychological suffering for so long, all that remained of me was an empty vessel, being tossed about on the ocean, gasping for air as I tried to keep my head above water. Paddling the great waters of depression, I often contemplated holding my breath and going under, where I would feel no more pain. Through this period, I received intensely strong dreams about tsunamis consuming me, seeing and hearing whales and being carried on their backs as I journeyed between the underworld and back. Within a 12-month period, my beloved nine-year-old cat and 14-year-old dog had died. While my marriage was ending, my father was ill with cancer. Alongside my siblings, we nursed our father for three long, agonizing years. He fought so bravely and, in the end, no matter our past conflicts and trials, all that mattered was that he left this world with every one of his children holding his hands and sending him off to the other world with more love than he felt in this world. I lost my relationship and my son went to college in the South, near all his friends, and stayed with his dad. It had been just me and Harry for 16 years, and so, with my father, my partner and my son all gone (or so it felt), I was left with a feeling of abandonment – the same feeling I would get as a young girl. Worthless, and alone.

But I love life and living so much; I have so much work to do and too many dreams to fulfil to stay down in that cave of sorrow. Though it was comforting, safe and its pull was strong, I clambered up the steep walls and out over the edge. And who was there waiting to blind me with her light? The moon. Every night I would speak with her, ask her what I should do. I burned candles, danced every day, burned herbs – mugwort and sage – and laid my naked body in her light so that her beams could fill all the empty spaces with white light and draw out the stagnant energy that had built up in me over years. I went only to nature and the moon for therapy, telling the trees of my grief, and my sheep often bore the weight of my torrent of tears. I was being bent and moulded, heated and shaped. I was stripping back, melting away, shedding the limitations of society and expectation, and stepping into myself, into love. Refined in the fires until the gold and strength returned again.

Returning to the Moon

It's the middle of the night and my grandmother won't let me sleep.

She keeps me awake and asks me why I rest. Why have I settled here in this realm?

My mother gently whispers to me. Why do I sleep alone in sorrow when I could be sleeping in her arms, surrounded by forests that will shield me, nurture me and give me shelter and peace? She beckons me out from the darkness, across great waters and along a path lit only by the moon to guide my return.

I'm going home.

Like a lost, wounded, hungry child who ran away to find her own path.

I'm done with corruption, greed and conformity, the selfishness of a broken world; the agony of witnessing the daily abuse of our sacred sisters, animals, land and water.

I'm going home, to my mother.

Mother made of soil and spirit. Moon and mountains. Sea and shelter. She is waiting to welcome me with open arms and hold me close to her breast. To cover me with wings like an eagle and in the silence of returning, I will feel her cool breath of wind on my cheeks once more.

I'm going home....

I fell in love with Grandmother Moon and her beautiful light when I was so lost and alone. I would look up to her and see her also alone in the sky and wonder how she must feel, but her light still shone. She came for me every night without fail. I now discover daily the huge historical importance of the moon on women's lives, from how she rules our hormones and cycles to our sacred monuments across the land that all align with the cosmos. Women and men can come home to the moon, our guide in the feminine dark.

In *The Great Cosmic Mother*, Monica Sjöö wrote that the moon, speaking through a tortoise, said to the African San Peoples, 'Tell them as I dying live, so they dying will live again.'

Phases, Wind and Water

I gained much wisdom about the moon and the role she plays in our lives from the Kanienkeha'ka. The knowledge is being kept alive and I share these teachings with you so that you may pass the truth of the moon on to your children and grandchildren.

According to the Kanienkeha'ka, when the moon is in her new phase and the face is hidden from Mother Earth, she is closest to the sun, and when something is very close to a heat source, it expands. So, in this phase, the moon is expanding, and as she expands, she gets pushed away from the sun and starts to rise. The way the moon moves away and rises is in the shape of a DNA coil, and because we are gravitationally linked, it causes her to gravitate around the Earth in an elliptical shape.

As she reaches the full-moon phase, when she is furthest away from the sun, she gets colder and therefore contracts. There are other things happening in the relationship between the moon, sun and

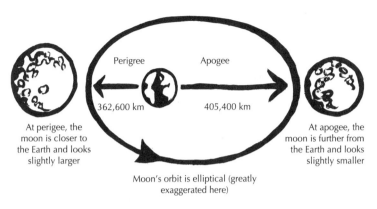

Perigree

Apogee

362,600 km

405,400 km

At perigee, the moon is closer to the Earth and looks slightly larger

At apogee, the moon is further from the Earth and looks slightly smaller

Moon's orbit is elliptical (greatly exaggerated here)

The moon teachings of the Kanienkeha'ka

Earth. As the Earth rotates on its axis, there is always one area on the planet going through a summer season and being warmed up. Heat on Earth causes condensation, which involves moisture rising into our atmosphere, especially early in the morning and late in the evening. This condensation is caught up in the solar winds sent out from the sun and pushed into the path of our Grandmother Moon in her full phase. The moon absorbs this moisture and continues rotating as she travels around the orbit of the Earth, back to her new-moon phase. She heats up again and expands, releasing the trapped waters back into the winds, which travel back to the Earth and the tides adjust. The cycle of wind and water release continues through each cycle of the moon around the Earth.

Imagine the moon being a sponge, with half of her being frozen – the side continually facing away from the sun. For example, in the full-moon phase, the side furthest away from the sun is in shade and completely frozen, but the side facing the sun lights up like a sponge, open and ready to absorb all the waters released from the Earth and carried to her on the solar winds. As she is travelling at about 10,000km/h (62,000mph), this force, called centrifugal force, is the mechanism that releases the waters back to the Earth. Centrifugal force originally kickstarted our Mother Earth into rotation, in perfect synchronicity.

Heartbeat

When the moon is halfway between her full and new phases, she is getting ready to open the valve to release the waters back out or on her return, receive them. This imagery is actually mirrored within our own hearts through the lunar valves! These two semilunar valves are located at the connections between the pulmonary artery and the right ventricle, and the aorta and the left ventricle. These valves allow blood to be pumped forwards into the arteries but prevent blood flowing from the arteries back into the ventricles.

So, with its expansion and contraction, the moon is just like our beating heart! One side of the heart is for expansion, the other side is for contraction and what sound does this make? Thud whoosh... thud whoosh... thud whoosh... well, this is the same sound and sequence of patterns that resound and echo throughout the universe between the sun, our moon and the Earth. The sound of the waters passing between the plants sounds like the beating heart of the universe.

The moon is therefore the beating heart of our Mother Earth and every living being on it. Anything that happens to her, happens to us and our hearts also. You know those times when you feel intense emotion, or food cravings, extreme thirst, irritability or when EVERYTHING seem to go wrong and everyone is angry, or you feel the need to be locked up in a padded cell? Then you stop, look up

Our ancient wisdom
is based on our
relationship with
our grandmother
the moon, Mother
Earth and the sun.

and notice what is happening in the cosmos. We are the cosmos, so you wonder why the moon affects things so much? Women heat up around the time of the new moon, when she is close to the sun. Notice it next time – maybe your sleep is disrupted and you're more restless.

Animals, I can testify, go wild in the full moon – Aeyla becomes more hyped and we have a monthly howling session (more for my benefit than hers)! Hospitals become overrun as women go into labour. So, if the moon can affect us that deeply, we should learn to harness that power and energy and use it for good. Women, you can become aligned with your purpose when your own moon, your menstrual cycle, lines up with the moon out there in space. Long ago, our sisters knew this and their menstrual cycles were in time with the moon cycles.

The reason we do not consider this much anymore is because we have forgotten our original instruction. Our ancient wisdom is based on our relationship with our grandmother the Moon, Mother Earth and the sun. Every woman is a filter for those waters and moons; our menstrual cycle keeps Mother Earth in balance. In this way, women bring purpose and direction that people must follow again – this is our original instruction. This is the integral, sacred, ancestral knowledge of the moon. It is a doorway to all the wisdom that is fading, because this knowledge challenges the narrative of modern science that declares our moon as a cold, dead, lifeless place. This is a lie, but they say this because they want everyone to agree to an economic assault on our moon. That assault is happening as we speak and is designed to extract all the precious life-force out of her. People don't know that she is alive, she is the beating heart, and so they don't realize that they're commodifying their own hearts.

My son had a dream about the moon when he was 15 years old. I had just begun to learn from the Kanienkeha'ka about how the big space exploration companies were seeking to colonize the moon. Harry woke me one morning and, as we lay next to each other, he told me in such detail that the moon was huge and was very close to the Earth now; it was almost close enough to touch. He said, 'it was filled with buildings, cities, lights and smoke everywhere', but he was still on Earth looking up. He looked around and saw that the Earth was a barren, brown wasteland and there was no one around, apart from one lady whose face he couldn't see, who led him away from where he was.

This dream demonstrates that our children can telepathically take on our thoughts and fears. He knew nothing of what I was learning about the moon; he didn't even know I'd contacted the Kanienkeha'ka people at the longhouse, yet he was dreaming about it – it was almost a premonition.

Turtle Shell

*'As the moon dieth and come back to life again,
so we also having to die, will live again.'*
Californian Indian prayer

Many First Nations teachings, including those of the Anishinaabe and the Haudenosaunee people, use the back of a turtle's shell as a lunar calendar. A lunar month is made up of 28 days as that is how long it takes for the moon to go around the Earth. This means that in one year (365 days), the moon goes around the Earth 13 times, giving us 13 lunar months with 28 days each. This pattern of lunar months in a year, and days in a lunar month, are represented on a turtle's shell. A turtle shell has 13 main sections (or scutes) surrounded by 28 smaller sections. These scutes represent the 13 lunar months in a year and the 28 days in a month.

Moons on the turtle's back

Over time, each moon was given a name and a story, often corresponding to the changes of weather and season, or the activities or planting you would do in each month. For instance, the hunter's moon marks the start of the season for hunting deer and elk.

MAKING MOON WATER

Make moon water to empower your spirit to keep strong and fuelled by the minerals, energy and light of the moon.

At the time of each full moon, fill a glass bottle with purified water and place it in the direct light of the moon's beams. Leave the bottle for two or three days, allowing the water to absorb as much of her nourishing light as possible, then speak your intentions over them. Speaking into water is powerful because your vibrations are echoed within the water molecules and will remain in your body when you consume them in the water. Water holds memory.

Your intentions, now embodied in moon water, will pass through each cell of your physical body when you drink it. So, consume the water over the next few weeks at periods when you need its nourishing light and hydration most, and then re-start again at the next full moon.

◇◇◇◇◇◇◇◇◇◇◇◇◇◇◇◇◇◇

PART III

Reclaiming
the Land

We need to take up the reins of the old ways, and re-learn those methods of working alongside our animal relatives. It is vital that we learn how to be custodians of the land again, to become more self-sufficient and ungovernable. Every year, I receive so many messages from people wishing to learn crafts and take part in my workshops, it is very encouraging. Many more people are realizing that our disjointed, ever more controlling, oppressive state is not working for the good of our health and communities anymore. People are looking for ways to be self-sufficient, to live off-grid, to home-school their kids and find land to support their dreams. But there are huge roadblocks in the system that are designed to make it impossible to live a life that's focused on thriving in your locality. Instead, we are fooled into a spiral of striving, working endlessly and putting into a system that only serves the rich. The powers that be make it a demoralizing prospect to live freely because they don't like the fact that when people are free, they take back their autonomy, in their mind, body and soul. Listen: You are a wolf, born to be free in the beauty of this world and all that Mother Nature has created for you to thrive in abundance and mutual connection.

Now is the time we should be living, but this means being reliant on ourselves and our own capabilities as cosmically made humans that long to be free of the shackles of conformity. Imagine having your own piece of land, where you could care for your animals and produce good-quality meat, and grow your own vegetables organically – a pipe dream, maybe? But some of us are proving it's possible. It's not without hardship, but this life of harmony with nature is a reward for rebuilding our ravaged planet. We're made to feel extreme guilt about the changes we need to make for generations to come – but does that mean our time now is worthless, sacrificial? For the good of humanity and our lives now, surely it's possible to achieve both.

The final part of my book is about healing wounds from our collective past and reclaiming ancient wisdom that has been stolen and hidden from us. I share tales and knowledge about the healing power of plants, as well as the cathartic power of land skills, such as traditional tanning, blade shearing for sheep and animal husbandry. Finally, I share the importance of a magical ceremony of reclaiming our blood rites as women and a ritual blood cleansing with the land, as well as how the scared stone monuments across the British Isles are our power source to plug us back into ancient communities and their wisdom. Time to reclaim our land, skills and ancestral wisdom.

We so desperately need to empower and embody women to be the beacons of light and truth again in our world today. If we open our hearts to the messengers of every kind – bird, stone, tree and wolf – they will come. They are waiting for us.

CHAPTER 18

An Ancient Fibre

Why not start a smallholding with a flock of sheep? In this chapter, I will demonstrate some key practical ways to do this and make a business from selling wool and sheep byproducts.

I love wool. I love the animal that produces wool. I wear wool, sleep on wool, cover my skin in the wax that coats and protects wool. I work with wool, in every way. I inhale wool; I use wool in my garden; I line my boots with it. The only thing I don't do with wool is eat it – well, not intentionally. This ancient water-shedding, sustainable, unique, home- and heart-warming fibre has kept us clothed since around 10,000BC. Wool tells a story about the very essence of survival and longevity.

It is suggested that the first domestic sheep were introduced into Britain by Neolithic settlers in around 4,000BC and that these were probably horned brown sheep, similar to Soay. Preserved wool from the Bronze Age appears to be from Soay and originated in the islands of Scotland.

Over time, these primitive sheep have endured harsh elements and, as a result, their wool has evolved to be resilient and hardy. Wool has a multitude of uses. It provides warmth in cooler climates and cools the body in warmer climates, by wicking away sweat (from both humans and sheep). Cultures across the globe have had long relationships with wool, from the Navajo Nation in Arizona to the desert-dwelling Bedouin people.

Sheep Breeds and Wool

There are more than a thousand breeds of sheep, each with its own unique wool characteristics, and texture can vary hugely. It can be soft enough for babies or coarse and brittle. Some fleeces are silky, some springy, some super fine, some short and some long and lustrous – all traits that are often reflected in the landscape from which the sheep originate.

The ancient, native British Herdwick sheep breed, for example, has lived on the fells of Cumbria for many generations. Herdwick flocks have nurtured and carved the land beneath them, regenerating a diversity of flora and fauna. I have worked with large flocks of these sheep and own a small flock myself, and when it comes to giving birth, their mothering traits are so clever. In the harsh, cold climate of the hills they will go to the prickly gorse bushes and nibble a small area away and push themselves in to give birth. This not only shelters the newborn lamb from biting winds and heavy snow, but it also disguises them from predators. Even though the adult sheep is slate grey, blending into the scree slopes of the fells, when the lambs are born, they are completely black. They then turn a lovely copper colour and then, after their first shear, they turn silvery grey. This is a clever evolutionary adaptation for blending into their natural habitat.

Herdwick wool is mainly used for rugs but the younger, softer wool is used for jumpers, blankets and hats. At the last count, I have about eight Herdwick sweaters; they are the warmest in my collection without doubt, although itchy.

The Boreray, from the islands of Orkney, has very similar wool to the Herdwick. A single fleece can carry various characteristics, and the kemp fibres are short, stubby, brittle, hollow hairs that are perfect for insulating the sheep in harsh mountainous regions.

Shetland and Icelandic sheep, meanwhile, produce dense, soft, short and long dual-coated fleeces. The dual coat of the northern short-tail breed is known as the tog and thel; the tog is the layer of long, coarser weatherproof wool above the thel, which is short, finer wool that sits next to the skin and is much warmer. These fibres, when spun together, make an exceptional multipurpose wool, known as Lopi yarn, and the earthy colours mirror the landscape where the sheep live.

A Multipurpose Material

Wool is very similar to human hair; the proteins and amino acids that are the building blocks of human hair, skin and fingernails are the same as those found in wool. Although some people claim to be allergic to wool, it's more likely to be an irritation caused by the lanolin within the wool, the plant matter left on the wool from grazing or the chemicals used in the treatment of the sheep throughout the year. Another possible cause of irritation may be the micron count of the wool. The micron count determines the fibre diameter; one micron is one-millionth of a meter. A Merino fleece will contain fibres with diameters as low as 10 microns, whereas a Herdwick fleece will have a micron count of 35 plus. So, the lower the number, the finer the wool; the higher the number, the coarser and more irritable the fabric. Wool's flexibility also makes it an amazingly durable fibre. A single wool fibre can be bent more than 20,000 times without breaking; whereas cotton will break after about 3,000 bends.

The endless list of qualities bestowed upon this magical fibre includes flame resistance: wool naturally contains nitrogen and moisture, which gives the fibre low flammability. Have you ever tried burning wool? It just sizzles and smells bad if it's still raw! Cotton burns at 225°C, whereas wool reacts at over 600°C. It is for this reason, alongside its insulating properties, that I clad out my camper van with huge sheets of felted wool. It's also a great mulch for gardens and keeps the snails at bay as they hate to clamber over its fuzzy fibres.

Wool has a self-sustaining microclimate; the air pockets in the wool fibres transfer odour and impurities from the skin into the air, so it is also self-cleansing. I almost never wash my wool garments; they just don't need it. Instead, hanging them out to air will suffice and save energy on washing. Wool has properties that stop bacteria from reproducing. It is also coated in lanolin, which prevents the skin from drying out. Lanolin is liquid gold in the cosmetic world and I extract it to make my own chemical-free body and hair products. Wool is strong and many well-made wool products will last a lifetime.

Woven into Memory

We are currently in a phase of diminishing the value and importance of wool. From being one of the most valued, treasured fibres and commodities across the entire globe for thousands of years, wool has almost overnight become a waste product – a burden, a nuisance destined for the incinerator or compost heap across most sheep farms. Despite its current state of poor value, wool has a colourful history.

When I look through a fleece of wool, it stirs up such emotion and passion in me. I often wondered why I love wool so much and found working with it so comforting, cathartic and enlightening, then I discovered that many of my family and ancestors on my father's side came from Foxford, County Mayo in Ireland. This is home to the world-renowned Foxford Woollen Mill, built on the banks of the River Moy and still thriving today! This craftsmanship, I'm certain, is embedded in my bones from a previous time, a past generation, a forgotten life that only now exists in my ancestry. The reason we follow certain passions in life and are drawn to certain areas, landscapes and animals, stems from what our ancestors witnessed, enjoyed and poured their hearts into and worked through. We are forever linked. Does this reflect anything in your own life – something you're drawn to or feel a passion for? Look back down your family line and you might just find traces of an unfinished story, waiting for you to rewrite the tale.

Everything has a memory, and this demonstrates how the things we touch and the people we meet become engrained in our DNA. For example, in a meeting of like-minded souls, an energy is exchanged; actual messengers from our receptors exchange data about the interaction and it becomes embedded within a person's psyche and cells. That energy exchange encodes within the network of fibres that make up our cells. When we die and are reborn, we still have that network and pass it through to the next generation.

Sheep and wool have shaped my life over the last 13 years. I run a thriving wool business now and my ethos is simple: I am a champion for the smallholder! I am also a champion for women, who are always told they're not strong enough or wise enough to be a farmer! I am an advocate for ethical regenerative agriculture that looks after our soils and animals. I own a small flock of primitive, rare breed sheep to preserve their heritage and produce slow-reared meat. They are a cross of northern short-tail breeds, including Icelandic, Shetland, Boreray, Hebridean and Manx. I also have Herdwick mountain sheep. They grow fleeces in a myriad of earthy colours. I hand shear and use the sustainable fleece to make wool rugs, tanned leather hides, felted sheep rugs and wild wool collars. As a guardian of traditional, ancestral skills, I'm teaching the lost ways and ancient crafts in workshops and retreats on how to raise animals, bring back value to wool and live more sustainably in harmony and connection with our land, wildlife, waters, moon, blood, deep feminine power and Mother Nature.

I believe that the way to heal our home from the destructive and throwaway society we live in, is to promote and live in a more sustainable, thoughtful and conscientious way, where everything we own and raise can be utilized efficiently and delicately, in balance with our planet. The sheep are sheared by me and I use the wool, backed by felt, to make wild wool rugs. These are my most popular product and sell out across the world. They are wild, rugged and yet incredibly soft, warm and durable, and every rug has a name and a story full of character that comes with it. They reflect the colours of the Earth in all its diversity and therefore every item is bespoke and individual.

I have been using my flock's resources in every way for several years now. I have taught hundreds of people over the years and it is so satisfying to see many go on to diversify their farm and set up their own wild wool rug businesses. This transference of skill from my hand to theirs is the way our grandmothers used to teach us.

We all want to save the planet and reduce waste, but it takes effort to sacrifice our consumerist nature. The change starts with each individual action. You could choose to support small businesses, where things are made with love. My business, and so many small cottage industries, used to be the backbone of our country and, I believe, will be again if we as consumers choose to support that change.

Harvesting Wool the Old Way – Blade Shearing

Blade shearing is said to be one of the oldest occupations in history and early farmers are believed to have used slender stone scrapers to shear sheep. Metal blades, like the ones I use today, were first recorded in an ancient Babylonian text. Then, in 1880, the electric system took over. So now the blade-shearing method is a dying art – and I'm all about saving those! Blade shearing uses a tool with blades that resemble large scissors to shear the wool from the sheep's body; they were possibly the origins of our multipurpose scissors. I have been shearing this way for 14 years now and I find it one of the most connecting, spiritual, fulfilling jobs of my calendar year.

Primitive breeds like mine can naturally shed their fleeces – well, most of them. But for welfare and rug-making reasons, I still shear. This prevents the sheep overheating and diminishes the chance of flystrike – an unpleasant infestation worth avoiding at all costs. Shearing also means I can harvest all the beautiful wool!

I have sheared with electric shears, which makes the job easier and quicker in many respects, but hand shearing is the best option for me and my sheep. Blade shearing is much less stressful for the sheep and is a cathartic ancient practice that improves the bond between sheep and shepherd, and is the most natural form of removing the fleece. Unlike electric shears, which take the fleece right down to the skin, blades can leave a good layer of wool on the animal with plenty of protective lanolin intact, so you can shear at any time of year. This layer protects the sheep from the elements through the bitter winter and unpredictable summer months.

During late spring and early summer, there is a natural break in the growth of the fleece, when the new year's wool comes through and the old breaks away – much like the changing of the seasons. Out with the old, in with the new…. This method isn't just for hobby farmers with a small flock – many hundreds of sheep can be sheared in a day with a good team, and much of my knowledge has been gained from Australian shearers where blade shearing is seeing a big revival.

Shearing day is a celebration – a harvest of my year's work. It is the day I gather the fleeces that will be made into rugs to support me and the sheep throughout the winter and the next year. Sadly, this ancient practice is yet another farm job that's seen as a chore. But I believe we can turn that around and celebrate our shearing day and make it a huge part of our calendar again. A festival of wool and sheep! That's my vision. Each year, I will invite the community, family, friends and anyone who wants to take part in the harvest of wool and cuddle the sheep. And at the end of the day, sticky and smelling of lanolin and sheep dirt, we will feast, drink and be merry.

I shear my flock of around 150 sheep by hand, then I shear for other smallholders who have such a small number of sheep that no one is willing to come out and set up their electric system. I don't just shear their sheep; I'll give them the knowledge, advice and tuition to take on the task themselves. I am mostly self-taught; I have travelled across the country displaying the craft at shows and fairs and, on one occasion, at a sheep-shearing festival in Loenen, in the Netherlands. It was a wonderful experience, apart from overhearing an old guy, looking down his glasses at me, ask, 'Doesn't she have sheep in England to shear?' Yes, misogyny crosses borders and, in a male-dominated industry, I overcome it by digging deep and not allowing judgement to define my role. Instead, I exceed their expectations. Women are making waves in the world of sheep and one thing we have in common is a very thick skin.

I use my skill to empower other women – and men – to take on these old ways and equip themselves to be less reliant on a system that's not designed for the benefit of most people. The only way I can see farming, and human civilization, surviving is by being more self-reliant. So, get every skill you can under your belt.

Farmers of old took note of the seasons and circadian rhythms. Things took time to make, grow, thrive; it was not the rushed, busy, overwhelmingly chaotic world we live in now. But in the past, farmers did not face the endless list of requirements, pressures, regulations, stipulations and abuse that they encounter today. I too realize that slow days don't make you money, but they do make you well, mentally and physically, and are much less stressful all round. I'll take awareness and tranquillity over success and wealth any day. Focus on the good and the beauty surrounding you every day, for the fear of time will wain and the love of the old ways will thrive again.

Talking of the abuse farmers get, we live in a world now where I am thought of as an animal abuser if I remove the wool from my sheep. Someone, somewhere, who most likely has never done a hard day's graft in their life, is telling me how to raise animals. There are organizations that spread false information, claiming that it is cruel to take an animal's wool for humans to wear. There are people who believe this, and I have to endure harassment from trolls online throughout the shearing season. I know it can appear to be stressful, unnecessary and barbaric to take an animal's fleece, but if we did not shear them, their hair would matt up with shit, mud and sweat over 12 months.

My hands and heart will continue to work tirelessly in this way of life, bound into the fibres of time, to keep this wool and work alive and thriving. All we need, as makers, shepherds and craftspeople, is for those who believe in the same vision to support the idea that wool is the greatest fibre on Earth. Shearing and taking an animal's coat is not a job, it's a feeling. It represents another co-dependent bond we have with an animal. The rediscovery of the old ways brings such emotion – a memory that you can taste, an alchemy of something so pure and spellbinding that it captures you in its web of barbed fibres and ignites a flame of inspiration that spirals into a flame of never-ending mystery. Women were the original shepherds, but like all other areas of history, mankind wanted us to forget our deep connection to the animals, land and fibres of nature. Tending animals and the Earth is our design; we are wanderers, nomads, herders. Once you dip one toe into this world, you will recognize the reflection you see staring back at you from a place where you were created, and remember who you are.

CHAPTER 19

Tanning Hides

Since the dawn of time, animal skins have been used for a variety of practical and economic reasons. They have been used for clothing, shelter, warmth, protection, communication and as a show of wealth. In most ancient and Indigenous cultures, tanning was done primarily by women, who were masters at processing animal skins into usable leather and furs. The tanned hides were made into dwellings, clothing, coracle boats and rugs. It was the First Nations people who developed a process of turning animal skins into usable material using animal brains to promote softness and pliability. Other animal parts were also used, such as the spinal cord, liver, bone marrow, fat or even vegetable matter, but brains seemed to be the most important ingredient.

In our modern society, we are disconnected from the animals we consume; I want to know what animal I'm eating and the life it has lived. I think we should all think that way; the way we used to when we lived much more closely and in harmony with the natural world. Back then, we didn't see ourselves as separate from the bison and deer; the role we played helped the health of the huge herds.

We took out the sick and old and, before any knife was drawn, herbs were picked from across the grasslands at peak harvest and seeds spread across meadows to keep the grass healthy and support the food source.

In basic terms, animals – our food source – were looked after through love and reverence, worship and respect. And in return these animals provided us with meat – clean, rich, healthy meat – and fat for making medicine and candles, as a base for herbal remedies, for use in cooking and for softening leather. Bone was used to make weapons to hunt, blades to butcher, jewellery to adorn, and tools to craft and build shelters. Skin was used to make leather for clothes, shoes and bags. Tendons produced sinew for sewing, and internal organs softened leather and provided food. The bladder, stomach and intestines were made into water-carrying pouches and for other unusual crafts. If an animal was killed, absolutely nothing was wasted; everything was used in honour of the animal's sacrifice.

Raw to Rebirth

Every person and culture has different methods to tan hides, formed through generations of work and experience. The remnants of this wisdom are now treasured and shared through books, workshops and social platforms across the world.

I have been tanning hides for nearly 10 years and in that short time, the interest and engagement in ancient skills has really rocketed.

'A society grows great when old men plant trees, the shade of which they know they will never sit in.'
Greek proverb

Where do we start? We go back to learning the skills and crafts we have always needed and spend days in the woods alone to rediscover our voice and strength, tanning hides, listening to the wind and making fire to awaken the sleeping soul. The smoke and ashes are of a lost world where indomitable women of a matrilineal line were the heart of the people. This world is contained within the magic of these primitive skills through woodsmoke and rebirth!

The Process: Start by Sourcing

Pretty much everything that has a hide is tannable, but many animal skins will not produce good results. The best and most common hides to tan are from rabbits, foxes and moles – in fact most small mammals – as well as coyote, skunk, fish, sheep, deer, cattle and bison. I have tanned many of these hides and often collected animals from the side of the road and salvaged the meat if it's still edible, or given the remains to the dogs, after removing the hide. You can tell if meat is good to eat by the smell. If it is rancid, your gut will thank you for not eating it. If it's got very little smell, it's likely a day or two old and still fresh, depending on the weather. It pays to carry a legal knife with you when travelling in your truck for occasions like this.

Sheep provide a hide that's relatively easy to tan and you can adapt the process to suit other hides as your interest, knowledge and experience increases. I'll give you the basic instructions to get started on your journey into converting animal hides into workable leather. This will, by no means, be a comprehensive, scientific guide to hide-tanning – that's another book to come. But I warn you, it's highly addictive!

The results can vary wildly due to so many external factors like weather, temperature, humidity, timescales, equipment and personal methodology. But if you follow this step-by-step guide, I'm certain you will settle down to sleep on a soft, cosy, warm sheepskin by the fire this winter.

You can source sheepskins from abattoirs where they will be glad for you to take them because, otherwise, they have to pay for them to be taken away as a waste product. In order to do this, though, you will need a Category 3 ABP (animal byproduct) licence, which is easily obtainable from the government body that deals with animal and countryside health. These regulations apply to the UK, so please check local regulations if you live elsewhere.

Hides collected from either an abattoir or the roadside need to be fresh, before bacteria set in and start to decay the skin. This is particularly important to consider when tanning sheepskins and keeping the hair on.

TANNING A HIDE

Once you've sourced a hide, it's time to start tanning.

Salting and Freezing

The hides can be stored fresh, by salting or freezing them. If you are salting the hides, do this as soon as possible after the hide has been removed, because as bacteria grow, the hide increases in temperature and the hair or wool becomes vulnerable to falling out. If this does happen, the hide is not wasted, it can still be used to make buckskin, or oak-tanned leather.

1. To salt the hides, cover them with a thick layer of non-iodized salt, so the skin is no longer visible.

2. Fold them in half and lay them flat on a pallet. The pallet should be raised slightly, at about 30 degrees from the ground, to allow for drainage of the liquid produced in the early stages of curing.

3. Once the liquid has stopped dripping, the hides will begin to dry a little. Then they can be stored in open drums or on crates or pallets without lids.

4. The hides can be re-salted a week or two later and left for up to a year if the room is well ventilated and free from vermin. I've actually had hides storing in salt for three years and, as long as they're hydrated well before tanning, they are fine.

I tend to leave mine to cure in the salt for two to four weeks. This makes removing the flesh and membrane easier and less slimy.

Preparing and Framing

1. When you are ready to tan the hide, hydrate it thoroughly, or defrost if your hides have been stored in the freezer. Dried, salted skins should be moistened for about 30 minutes until pliable. Do not soak them for too long in case the fur comes out. For the next stage you will need to remove the flesh from the hide.

2. Use a fleshing knife; a long thin knife that can be straight or curved, with an edge bevelled at 45 degrees and slightly blunted so that it doesn't cut the skin when fleshing. Place the hide over a wooden beam and use the knife to push downwards, away from your body, removing all the large lumps of flesh and membrane.

3. Next, place your de-fleshed hide into a frame – a square shape with reinforced corners to give it stability. You could make a

natural frame with long coppiced hazel rods that can be bent over and tied, or simply tack the hide onto a pallet to stretch out the fibres.

4. Use a leather awl to make holes about 7.5cm (3in) apart all around the perimeter of the hide.

5. Then, take some twine or thick nylon and thread it through each hole and over the edge of the frame to tie the hide up tight. String the top and bottom of the frame first and finally each side until there is no slack.

6. If space is an issue, you could omit the framing stage and soften the hide over a stake instead, but this method doesn't always produce a soft leather. Soften the skin by gently pulling, kneading and manipulating it with your hands if you omit the frame stage.

7. Then, apply the sheep-brain solution; I use a single brain per hide. (Eggs can be used instead of brains, as they contain lecithin, the compound useful in softening the fibres of hide. I use six egg yolks, with a little warm water or oil, for an average-size sheepskin.) The brain can be applied alone or mixed with various emulsifying solutions. Sometimes, I use oil (any kind will work). The brain is easier to spread if it is blended, and I add the oil at this stage – a couple of shot glasses full. If you can't blend it in a machine, then use a pestle and mortar to bash it up.

8. Then, work the egg or brain mixture into the skin. Take some time doing this as it will improve the outcome. Consistently rubbing in the mixture will create friction, which in turn warms the hide and opens the network fibres of the skin, allowing the oils to be pushed in and trapped.

Drying and Softening

The hide is now ready to be dried and softened. Never dry the skins in the sun or near a hot fire; they should dry slowly in cool shade. Long wool sheepskins can take several hours to dry on a cool day, but on a warm summer's day they will dry quite rapidly, so work quickly to avoid the skin becoming too hard and brittle before it dries.

1. Soften the hide as it dries by working a blunt wooden stick into every area, paying particular attention to the thicker areas around the neck and rump. Take care around the thinner sections under the arms as this tears easily dependant on the age of the sheep. The younger the sheep, the thinner the hide; this also applies if their wool is thick and very long, like my Icelandic cross Shetland breeds.

2. Keep breaking down and manipulating the fibres, working in the drying brain solution at the same time. You'll notice the colour change as it dries, from a raw blue to a yellow-white. If the wool is wet, it needs to dry as soon as possible to avoid hair slippage.

3. When the hide is fully dry, and your arms are burning with all the softening, you can take it out of the string and off the frame.

Smoothing and Smoking

1. Take care with the final tanning stages to create a beautiful and durable finish.

2. The hide can then be smoothed over, using a pumice stone to remove remnants of membrane and give a good finish. You could leave the hide in this condition, but I always waterproof it to prevent the hide hardening if it gets wet.

3.   To waterproof the hide, it needs to be smoked. Smoke contains all kinds of chemicals that will seal in the tanning solution and ensure softness. It seals the tan and leaves a beautiful colour with a waxy layer of protection over the hide. It also smells of woodsmoke
and nostalgia for days gone by. So, build a fire and let the flames die down so you have some strong hot coals glowing. I make a tepee frame with a few wooden poles over the coals and hang the hide inside.

4.   Then, I cover the tepee with a tarpaulin and seal it to prevent smoke escaping except through a small hole at the top, which draws the smoke up past the hide. I hang up to four hides at time in the tepee by clipping the edges together with pegs.

5.   Once everything is in place, you can add rotting wood, known as punky wood, to the embers. Punky or rotting wood is found on dying or dead fallen trees (it should not be wet). You can use various sources of wood to give different colours. I tend to use oak, birch or spruce. This rotten wood should be chopped or crumbled into small pieces and added to the coals gradually a bit at a time. You will see the smoke emerge and it will take two to four hours to give a good coverage.

6.   Once the hide is smoked, you can either rewash it or simply brush out the wool and trim any crusty edges with a Stanley knife.

◇◇◇◇◇◇◇◇◇◇◇◇◇◇◇◇◇◇◇

This is a simple and effective tanning method to get you started. As you become enveloped in the ancient art of hide tanning, you may experience a vibration within your hands – a remembering, a revival. In everything there's a door, a portal to transport you to a place of metamorphosis.

Medicine of the Hands

Hide tanning in today's world is pure medicine.

This craft is a metaphor for our earthly transformation.

Flesh out all the wounds and waste.

Soak up the oils, knowledge and enlightenment.

Then, using all you have learned, you need to be stretched. Tested, strengthened.

If you can't hold out, endure and resist, you won't be given the great gifts waiting to be bestowed upon you by the universe.

Finally purified, sealed and protected, skin and flesh made new, we come through the fire and return in a true pure form, built to last for eternity….

CHAPTER 20

The Stones

We are the people of the stones, and it was through my meeting with the stones, particularly those at Avebury and Silbury Hill in Wiltshire, that I had two of the most transformational experiences of my life. I discovered a relationship with a place – a belonging you can only reach when you pass over the portal of the ancient stones.

The publication of two wonderful books by Michael Dames, *Silbury Treasure: the Great Goddess Rediscovered* (1976) and *The Avebury Cycle* (1977), revealed that this part of Wiltshire is the ancient sacred centre and represented the pregnant womb of the Neolithic Mother. According to Monica Sjöö in *The Spiral Journey* (2018), Michael's books were ridiculed by much of the patriarchal academic community who would not admit that the Neolithic culture of the scared stones was created by women and that women were both the ancient farmers and shaman/astronomers.

In this ancient landscape, I found the Great Mother Goddess and saw laid out before me, across the land, her body built in monuments: Silbury Hill, the womb of the Earth surrounded by the moat of her amniotic waters, and the West Kennet Long Barrow, her portal cunt where death and life emerge.* I am forever changed because of these places. The waters of life flow out all around and up to the sacred spiral and stone circles of Avebury. If we want to delve into the underworld and become a seer, we must be prepared to be raised up, dug up, broken apart, torn down and held up again like a monolith.

Silbury Hill

Silbury Hill is around 4,400 years old and is the largest prehistoric mound in Europe at 30m (98ft) high and 160m (525ft) wide. Up there, on my first visit to the mound, I felt the Earth's pain and rage, her great love and deep sorrow. Only on my return home would I discover more about where I had been standing, in awe and mesmerized. This mound had been entirely made by hand, using chalk and earth dug out over hundreds of years. It is estimated to have taken over 4 million hours to build the spectacle.

I discovered Monica Sjöö's art and writing about Silbury Hill and Avebury after I visited them. About 40 years after her first experience with Silbury, Monica wrote about the transformative experience she had there, in the year of my birth, 1978, in *Spiral Journey*.

Our experiences at the site were so similar, with Monica finding herself taken over by feelings of enormous grief. During her visit, she sees a notice declaring the monument closed due to erosion – shut off by barbed wire, surrounded by water, she feels the mound crying through her as she sits feeling at one with the Mother.

---

* *Cunt* is the Old Norse word, whereas *vagina* is the Latin. I have used the former because it is the original; modern society has made it into a cuss word.

Grief pours from her for lost women cultures, for the death of her land all around.

If the timings are right, she says, being fully present at the site can cause profound change in a person's psyche.

It always takes me a little while to recover after seeing the stones. They make me have intense dreams and fill me with energy, but leaving and coming back to 'normality' takes some adjusting.

Places like this are shrouded in mystery and atmosphere; you can't help but be moved when there. They stagger me because in our stress-filled, fast-paced, material world, they are reminders of a time when people worshipped their dead and living so much that they left an eternal mark on the landscape to remind us of who we are, who we were and what we valued and loved: the Goddess, our Mother, our ancestors.

Our future lies in our past.

If you journey here, it will change you if you let it, if only as a reminder of how short our time here is and to amplify what's truly important in our life – the land we are born from and the ones we love, past and present. I am a searcher, always searching for the meaning of life; I never settle for the now. It's hard to put into words what I experienced in the presence of these great stones.

Avebury

Going to the Avebury Neolithic landscape, which is full of monuments, stone circles and places of ceremony, was like stepping back in time to a place where community, energy, and connection with the land and elements was commonplace and essential for survival. The people who created the monuments knew the divinity that flowed through all things; they lived in tune with the seasons, the cosmos and the cyclical movement of nature.

The history and energy here was tangible and astounding! It was the winter solstice when I walked in the freezing cold, touching every ancient sarsen stone. Each touch felt like a bolt of energy surging through my flesh. I walked barefoot, in awe of the spectacle and, as darkness fell, eventually settled on a particular stone. I sat beneath the towering sandstone and warmth surrounded me like a cloak as I sat in ceremony until midnight. In my terms, this ceremony means speaking with my lineage, the stone people, from whom I am descended. I asked them to be with me always; to give me strength and guide my path. All the time, I was protected and watched over by the moon above. It was without doubt the most powerful soul connection I've ever had. I could have stayed there forever, for it's the closest I've ever felt to being fully accepted in this world.

West Kennet Long Barrow

My visit to West Kennet Long Barrow, a burial chamber, was equally profound. There never seems to be another soul around when I go to these places. I don't know if that's true or if I don't notice anyone because I'm so entranced with the magic and aura surrounding me. Standing beside such a huge and ancient monument to death, you feel a combination of reassurance, of safety, with trepidation and uncertainty.

The sun was low in the sky when I visited, and clouds were building up across the sprawling landscape of the Wiltshire downs, with Salisbury Plain in the distance. Before I went into the chamber, I walked the perimeter of the long barrow, knowing with every step that this cemetery was built in honour of the people who lived here more than 5,000 years ago. I became mesmerized with thinking about the way they lived, clothed in wool and leather, with sheepskin shawls and barefoot. They lived in communities that studied the cosmos every night, hunted wild animals on the plains around me and picked flowers that are still at my feet, descended from ancient seed. They cut up clay for pots and whittled flint tools from the abundance of chert found scattered around these hills. What did they eat for supper? Where did they take a crap and wash? What were their death ceremonies like? Would you want to live in their world or our modern one?

I reached the end of the barrow and lay down over the chamber that sheltered my ancestors. I wasn't well at this time, that's why I had gone there, for help. I was suffering from an incurable (so western medicine says) disease with flare-ups that were scary and exhausting. I can't help but cry in moments like this; there's a spirit that descends and holds me, making me feel heard.

The sun was bright pink as she kissed the horizon and my eyes were fixed on the clouds above as I began to speak out. I pleaded to be free from illness and gain clarity of mind again as the clouds started to part. In the middle there were darker clouds and the edges were white and churned up like rocks on a shoreline.

The vision that emerged was a mirror reflection of the land below – the land I was lying upon. A chamber in the sky developed and I'd go so far as to say that I saw a portal that only can be seen from this location, on this day, when you're crying out for help from your father, grandparents and beyond. I simply asked for healing within my body, for my high level of thyroid hormones to regulate themselves back into balance again. The cloud portal closed and I walked back to the end of the barrow.

I went through the cold entrance enveloped by mammoth stone plinths into the darkness. With one foot in each world, I kissed the stones and grounded my feet on the bare earth. I took a small jar of my blood out of my pocket and painted a spiral, similar to those found in Neolithic art, on an inner wall of the chamber, as many women before me have done in honour of our link to the spirit, creator, moon and death itself.

Two weeks a later, I went for a blood test to monitor the illness in my body. The last reading gave dangerously high levels of thyroid hormones, but this time the doctor was more surprised than me to see my levels had stabilized within the normal range. I smiled down to my bones and thanked the ancient ones for intervening.

If you go to these magical places, don't go as a tourist; go with expectation and with the intention of feeling them. Allow their energy, thick with intense vibration, to penetrate you. Trust that there is more to this world and your life than that which you can see and explain. The best things that will ever happen to you in your life will be a mystery and highly unexplainable in the physical realm. Seek and ye shall find.

Blood and Moon

The womb is our compass for revival. Blood from a woman is not dirty, or demonic – it is our superpower. I embarked on learning about our sacred flow and how it rises and falls with the moon and the tides. This knowledge brought me back, back to the web within

If you go to these magical places, don't go as a tourist; go with the expectation and with the intention of feeling them. Allow their energy, thick with intense vibration, to penetrate you.

my womb that links me back to every woman before me and our connection to the Earth.

The first moment I saw my bleed differently was when a Wolf Clan representative told me how this monthly power of mine was sacred. He was a man, but he had been raised in the ways of the matrilineal line. No woman had ever expressed this idea to me; they were under the same spell, believing it was an inconvenience, a nuisance, a pain that they, like me, spent all our time cursing and wishing away. I regret so deeply the years, decades, I spent with no memory of its first arrival or any initiation into its great purpose and how we should care for ourselves during this time. Instead, the theme was, 'Whatever you do, DON'T tell anyone, just shove a pad up there and get on with it.' And, as for tampons, those chemical-filled, plastic sticks may be toxic for some women (but there are organic alternatives). Although sanitary towels came on to the market in the 1920s and tampons the 1930s, it was not until recently that researchers have begun to use blood instead of water to test their safety and efficiency. Why not look at alternatives that don't harm you or our environment and don't waste your precious blood.

I wear a moon cup that is made of silicone and creates a vacuum that minimizes leaks as it collects my blood. If you're wondering why you should be collecting your blood, I'll tell you. Every month you release an egg, a life-form that has your iron-rich intelligence, and what do we do to honour those precious eggs? When we have no use for them, we teach our young life-givers to flush them down the toilet into oblivion. I know our bleeds can be painful, but we're looking at them in the wrong way.

Giving life to another soul is the greatest honour of the life-giver. To grow life, women need to prepare; we prepare in conjunction with the moon who regulates our cycles. In each of our eggs is a cell which can bring to life not only a daughter, but a granddaughter to continue our line – just as you were in your grandmother's womb when she was pregnant with your mother. Hence, the names of: Grandmother Moon, Mother Earth, Daughters of the Earth. If you feel called to save your blood, what will you do with it? Our ancestors would have looked after the women and young women when they were bleeding, cooking for them, helping to raise their children, massaging their backs and warming their feet until the phase had passed. That's how we should be treating our bodies and minds when we menstruate. But we don't live in communities of grandmothers; instead we have to grit our teeth, plough on, grimace through the cramps, make meals, clean the house and not moan about it. That's what this society we live in now expects of us. Well, it's no wonder we're all burning out.

So next time your moon comes (and do call it your moon; 'period' is a term given to it by men), take a jar, label it and fill it with blood from your moon cup or any other sanitary product you use, and add water to wring it out. Freeze it, then take it to all the sacred areas on the Earth you love: a monument, a forest, the river or your garden. Then, pour the 'good mind' of your blood back into the earth and root your intention into the ground and waters to restore peace and love, instead of fear and corruption.

A Ceremony on Silbury

I shall tell you of my ceremony up on Silbury Hill. This day was one of the most important and transformational of my life, and I feel called to share it because this moment was born through desperation and agony at our dying world. We are on the edge and

I feel it deeply every day. That feeling brought me back to a powerful place of reimagining – the womb of these isles, the Great Goddess, Silbury Hill.

I drove along the windy road on the eve of the true winter solstice, when we enter the longest night – a time of rupture, where all wounds are exposed and weeping, ready for change and rebirth. The anticipation of seeing Silbury again was rewarded with a welcome from six red kites all soaring above me as I finally caught a glimpse of her overwhelming presence and beauty. That night, I would be up there with her awaiting the return of the light.

In the early hours of darkness, I walked across the crisp frosty fields with only the moon to guide me towards the base (and amniotic moat) of the mound. As I walked, I sang (badly) the lost words blessing. Not a soul was around as I clambered up her steep face in freezing temperatures, and as I reached the top I knelt down, out of breath with my heart racing, and said, 'I made it Mother, I made it.'

I carried my sheepskin for warmth, my drum, a single swan feather – representing the Goddess – and my bottled blood, alone and guided by a distant memory of blood and bone. I set down my things and felt an immense warmth up there despite the temperature. The light started to break on the horizon and I spoke out to our Mother Earth, and I poured my collected blood into her belly so that my seed would forever be there with her and with the spirit of my ancestors who built the mound in honour of her.

By now the sky was beginning to light up in myriad colours – purple, blue, pink and orange – and I set down my bag and sheepskin bed and began to drum to the sun's approaching dawn.

This display developed into the most breathtaking and enchanting spectacle that I have EVER seen. I couldn't help but weep at her beauty and, in those moments, I felt she understood why I was there.

The mind cannot comprehend such beauty in a world so ravaged by corruption, war and pain. I went to Silbury in desperation, not just for me, but for a world our children will inherit. She knew – the moon behind me and the sun in front to hold me up on the belly of our Sacred Mother…. If there was ever a time to warrior up and regain my strength it was in that moment, and up there I knew exactly what I was here to do, with her strength and guidance.

I set my intention in the chalk and dirt of the monument at that moment. I spread the blood across the earth with the swan feather and poured out my heart to the feminine warriors and life-givers of my line to be the beacons, to bring back the truth to this world. I called on them to help us to remember who we are, why we are here and for the strength needed to change the course of history in such a fractured, disconnected, desperate world.

I prayed for my son, my family, for all my sisters not only by blood and for humanity. I then held the feather to the light and swore to spend the rest of my days in this realm fighting for her and the freedom of women. The drum sealed my ceremony as the dawn came with an indescribable display of light, colour and beauty, and in that glorious, visceral place of the gods I knew she was honouring me for crying out to her.

I am forever changed. I have no idea what led me to do what I did that morning, but I feel it happened because I was fulfilling a cry I made to her when I was eight years old, from the top of a hill near my childhood home, where I had declared that when I grew up, I wanted to heal the world *(see Chapter 4)*. This is my path, now and forever.

The Blood Ceremony

I smear myself with the blood of my womb, across my face like war paint, across my heart and belly, because my wild feminine nature tells me I should. I have poured my fresh blood in almost every corner of the British Isles and also on Turtle Island. This means a part of me will always exist within the DNA of those places, absorbed into the soil and mycelium of the underworld. This is how wolves leave their scent, and women can leave their mark over the territory of their home. So, it seems, the older we get the more savagely wild we become.

I am from the dirt, from the waters filled with blood, from women who bled and danced before our ancient grandmother, the moon. Once I would have been terrified to expose my wildness, but now I have shed enough layers of inhibition to share it and run freely with the wolves!

We need more rawness in the world. Less fakeness, less filtering, less influencing. More reality, more relatability, more vulnerability. We need to be less self-driven in purpose, more often baring our souls and the truth of human nature. This is me at my core. This will be all of us if only we could return to nature and live, once again, wild and untamed.

So, you can do the same. Nourish your garden, house plants, hearth and home, wherever you feel called. But I strongly suggest, at least once in your life, take your blood to the sacred stones of Neolithic

Britain for a surge of heightened power bolts through your hands from those ready to welcome you home.

PERFORMING A BLOOD CEREMONY

First, speak out your thanks:

> *I give my thanks to our Grandmother Moon – the beating heart of our Mother Earth who regulates the flow of all the waters – she who has given us blood.*

> *I give thanks to our Mother Earth – the physical embodiment of the Great Mother who gives of herself to create us – the mother of us all; she who has given us our body.*

> *I give my thanks to all the women, from the newest-born baby girl to the eldest grandmother, as they are all the mothers of our nations and should be honoured for their sacred title of life-givers – you give us direction.*

> *We pledge to the Great Spirit, to protect the Great Spiral of Creation and defend our Grandmother Moon.*

Add your own words after this and the intentions you'd like to lay in the ground with your blood.

Then take a feather – any feather is fine as it represents the air, but if you have the goddess feather of the swan, even better. Spread your blood across the feather and speak out your heart, your pain, your wishes as you coat the grasses and soil with the feather while moving in an anticlockwise direction in a rite of passage that should have happened on the day you first bled. Reclaim menarche (your first bleed) one feather, blood and sunset at a time!

◇◇◇◇◇◇◇◇◇◇◇◇◇◇◇◇◇◇◇

CHAPTER 21

Grandmother Oak

Grandmother Oak sits proudly in an ancient hedgerow a few miles from me. I came into her presence 11 years ago. The first time she made an imprint on me was when I was at college and my son was young. I was in a very different place back then, stuck in a mindset of imprisonment and people pleasing. My consciousness, although great, was a fraction of what it is now; age and Neolithic stone encounters, it seems, soften the heart.

Some trees just have this mesmerizing presence; you're drawn to them like a granddaughter drawn to her grandmother with a sweetie jar in her hand. I would walk past the oak most days for a year, and I just remember her presence and beauty. I could feel her energy long before I arrived at the base of her elephant foot-shaped trunk. This was the start of my journey to becoming a shepherd and custodian of the land.

She called me back a few years ago, when my sheep were grazing a meadow a few miles away. I walked past her branches most days and she carried me through so many trials during this period. I would share my life with her in a few seconds when I stopped briefly to hold her bark. She must have seen the change in me over those two years. She witnessed the loss of my father – the days I would cry uncontrollably with my head against her trunk, my tears nourishing her roots, pleading with her to help my father live. I wanted her to heal the cancer that ravaged his body like an uncontrollable bush fire. She held me through the drawn-out end of a long and damaging relationship. She supported me through many turbulent times and did not judge or belittle me when my livelihood was falling apart.

Later, when I was unwell, I pleaded with her for healing. I placed my head, heart and womb against her bark; my arms embracing her rough, gnarled crevices, exchanging energy and aligning DNA. Moths would hide beneath her great sheltering boughs, camouflaged until I discovered them as I stared at the scars on her trunk.

The Healing Tree

Do you have a particular tree that you're drawn to – one that captivates you and has watched your life unfold? If not, then go out into the woods and see which one you take a second glance at, then place your hands on, and lean your heart against, the bark.

A PROCESS OF RELEASING PAIN

1. Focus on the ailments within your body, the area that needs healing, the organ or muscle, joint or cell.

2. Close your eyes and focus on the colour of your pain, on what needs healing. Visualize it leaving that area and being drawn through your body, up along your right shoulder and down

through your arm and hand, following the same course of blood flowing through your body out from the heart.

3. When the colour reaches your hand, imagine it flowing into the tree and leaving your body.

4. Move around your body to the areas that need healing and repeat the practice.

5. Always give thanks to the tree when transferring your pain.

Tree networks are the epitome of a community and have so much to teach us about what we need in order to be well nourished and supported. They communicate through their roots and house many different spiritual and magical entities. Memories and environmental events are stored within their network, and it's believed some memories are passed on to offspring to warn them of attacks. Some trees even sacrifice themselves to preserve the community or younger trees.

I don't know if you've ever hugged a tree for longer than 20 seconds, but it has always had a profoundly positive effect on my emotions and spirit, and scientific studies have proven this effect again and again. But do trees respond to us and our love? Every living being emits and responds to frequency and energy, yet we do not function along the same timeframe. So, when we hug the tree and it feels like we get no response, maybe it is because we're not there long enough to feel it. Trees are slow, gentle giants, not busy bees obsessed with time. It is not inconceivable that several hours after we have left the tree, she responds – maybe by rustling her leaves, like a shudder of warmth and a dopamine rush that hugging someone we love brings.

Although I don't think we should believe something just because it's been proven 'scientifically', studies have shown that trees have a heartbeat. The tree's girth has been measured over a period of hours and it has contracted and expanded, pushing its internal waters to the crown and canopy of the tree. It has a heartbeat that works over a longer cycle of many hours, unlike our faster, distinguishable beat. Trees give us life. They breathe out what we breathe in, and they breathe in what we breathe out. Interdependence between these living organisms explains why there is so much reverence and respect for trees across most Indigenous communities.

Many words for body parts in the Kanienkeha'ka language relate to trees. For example, the word for toes (*ohiakwira*) translates as roots, and fingers (*tesasonhsasonteronnion*) as saplings. In their culture, they say we were all born through the trunk of our mother.

I have now planted hundreds of trees across the world through my wool business. For every sale I make, I pay a percentage to the TreeSisters, who work with communities across the world restoring lost habitats *(see page 237)*. This is how I redress the balance of using a truck and trailer and sending out rugs to homes across the world.

So, I hope you will seek out a tree that can hold you through life's storms and successes. Make the forest your destination, or if you live in a city select a tree from those lining the streets, or look in a park or garden. Take the time to notice her branches and where they hang, smell the sweet decay of fallen leaves and breathe the scent of the musty rich lichen that clings to her bark. Listen to the wind that speaks to you through her leaves, through the whistling branches. Tell her the good and the bad of your life; she can be your permanent, grounded journal that will continue growing your dreams into the earth long after you have gone.

CHAPTER 22

The Restorative
Energy of Plants

The medicinal properties of plants saved me and my body from a chronic autoimmune disease and heart complications. A few days after my father's death, I was hospitalized. Since then, I've been on a journey of learning about my body and which herbs I need around me to heal from these conditions naturally, avoiding mainstream pharmaceuticals. When I was adopted into the nation of the Kanienkeha'ka, I was told that if I ever became sick, I should call out the name nature knows me by, Iekawehatie, and nature will bring to me the medicines I need to heal.

Many plants have helped, but mugwort and hawthorn have been my plant allies through a tough time – and they can be for you, too. We have lost so much plant wisdom from our witch ancestors; it's our responsibility to bring it back in honour of them and in defiance of our patriarchal oppression. I don't claim to be a herbalist, but I am a woman of plant medicine with the knowledge of a thousand witches behind me, helping me to resurrect a whisper of wild healing. I don't mind admitting that I speak to plants!

Butterfly

She is called Graves' disease and she has come to bring me a message. This isn't just a cold, or seasonal flu that comes and goes. This is something defined by modern-day science as being chronic. I fucking hate that phrase. Nothing is forever, not even life itself. My body is a host to a cell that has become confused, lost its way, its purpose, but that cell is part of *me*, she is mine, intricately and beautifully made and I love her, and I want to do all I can to help her get better. She is part of my normal endocrine system and she plays a vital role in my body to balance my hormones delicately.

If any of our hormones become even slightly out of balance, the repercussions can be felt throughout the entire network of pathways, receptors, messengers and magical movers of information throughout the body. My confused cells tell my pituitary gland that my thyroid gland isn't producing enough hormones and so a message is sent to the thyroid gland located in the neck. Once the thyroid receives the message, she starts to replace the thyroid hormones.

But the message is wrong, there are enough; she is working just as she should, but in confusion. My body now has too many thyroid hormones and is out of balance. This continues until other areas of my body are affected, like my heart and bones.

The thyroid gland is so beautiful that she is in the shape of a butterfly. The butterfly is the master of transformation, representative of rebirth; she is the most distinctive creature in the animal kingdom.

In the cocoon of stillness, the most enchanting miracle of beauty and resilience is about to be birthed from the darkness – from death to life she emerges in a cycle forever entwined with the laws of the universe. What if this is happening in my body and she is waiting for me to acknowledge that I must be in the cocoon; I must be still in the dark so that my wings can grow. Every seven years, every cell in our body is replaced and we become a new version of ourselves.

It was 15 December 2019, three days after the death of my father, that I found myself in hospital with a racing heart and I was terrified that I was dying. Before this day, I had never had any serious illness – actually, I had the worst strain of bacterial meningitis when I was 18 but that is but a distant memory now! Why do I suppose the doctor diagnosed me with broken heart syndrome as she sat by my bed, gazing at me with her big, gentle, caring eyes? I visualize now a scenario where I was handed a bag to carry at the age of 11, when my parents separated, and I carried it on my back for 30 years until the day my father died, and I could lay it down. That bag holds a library of tales and copious amounts of stuff that I shall lay out for you, for you might recognize bits of it – they may also be in your bag. When you least expect it, the universe will send you a sign that you've carried your burden long enough and you can lay that weight down.

Emerging from the Chrysalis

Fear and anxiety are in my bag. My heart is strong; she has been through so much with me. We do not shy away from facing our demons and the demons are healing us from the things that wish to keep us bound up and afraid. For if we are afraid, we are not powerful in this world. We are just existing, but our purpose is not to exist, *it is to live* – fully, wholeheartedly, passionately, enthusiastically, vibrantly, forever evolving and growing, and glowing and flourishing into every single combined version of who we have been and will become through our lives. But lately, I stopped doing things for fear of getting ill or being away from home and comfort. Nothing in my life has challenged my mental health as much as losing my father.

Some people mistakenly believe that struggling with our mental health means that we're weak, incapable or a failure in some way. If you try to eradicate depression and fear from your life, it will only reappear later down the line and probably with greater consequences. *But* you can overcome these ailments, even if it means that through every dark, terrifying day, you choose to find one good thing you're grateful for – even if it's as simple as the fact your legs work, your heart beats, the sky is blue or there's milk in the fridge. That *one* good thing will often be so powerful in your mind when you choose to focus on it, that the heavy stuff loses its power over you. If you can, stand in front of the mirror each night before you go to sleep and tell yourself you made it through another fucking hard day and survived.

I have suffered with anxiety for most of my life, from the age of 14 until a couple of years ago. Now, I'm beyond letting that negative self-talk dictate my world. I'm taking it back, day by day. That doesn't mean I don't feel agonizing misery at times, but I am not staying in that pit for long. I have too much to live for, to fight for – for my son and every child I wish I'd given birth to but didn't, because I was deprived of them through the hands of another's torment.

I don't believe in glossing over life with trite phrases like 'love and light', 'peace' and 'live, laugh, love'. Life is suffering, walking the path of broken glass, finding jewels along the way. But I don't believe we stay broken; we repair and heal wounds every day and we must cherish those short moments of happiness and calm.

I walked away from the hospital after my dad passed hoping that would be the last I'd see of hospitals. Time to breathe and start again... but my heart had other ideas.

I never expected to be in hospital myself a few days later.

Trauma has visited me many times, on many occasions, and on each one I have found ways to get through, to stand against the adversity, to learn the lesson it brings and to move on with acceptance and change. But this lesson involved the most important thing in my life, my heart, that which gives me life every day and which I take for granted – we all do.

My heart asked me if it could give in; it hurt too much, not just for this season, but for the many things I hadn't dealt with and truly felt their loss. I have always felt invincible, strong, determined and I have expected my body to keep up with my spirit.

How we take our daily life for granted: the fact that we'll wake up every morning and our heart will still be beating to the same incredible, mesmerizing rhythm, as always. My heart became weak, but my spirit became stronger. This trial led me to the plants and their abundant medicine and for that, I'm eternally grateful to my body and my butterfly-shaped thyroid.

Plant Medicine

Now is the time to reclaim the wisdom hidden from us, the plants that are waiting to be rediscovered and used in our healing. We are sick, our Earth is sick, but we have all we need right in front of our eyes. We just need to rebuild those libraries of knowledge stolen from the women who had to bury it to survive. I honour every witch and woman who risked her life to remember this knowledge so that we might heal. The messages from the other world come in the form of plants and healing. You do not need to be a trained herbalist to treat yourself or others. We should share our experiences, wisdom and medicine with each other. For if we can bring healing to our bodies without western medicine, imagine how the mighty pharmaceutical companies will fall. In order to do this, we need to reclaim our land, which was also stolen from us by the establishment.

The time to reclaim our land to grow our food, herbs and future is now. How do we do this? We pursue everything that makes us self-sufficient outside the current economic system. Learn, learn, learn the ways of old – the ones we used to survive for thousands of years. You know, the time before supermarket devils took over our diet and wallet. I'll keep saying it: Learn to hunt, learn to skin animals and utilize their entire bodies, waste nothing and honour everything along the way.

Reintroduce gratitude and ceremony into your daily life, welcoming the sun each morning and kissing her goodnight, and welcoming the moon rise, kissing her goodnight at dawn. Share your abundance back with the earth: grow plants for medicine, grow vegetables and fruit, and learn to preserve it all. Make your life count for *you* and your family and, if you can build one, for your community.

Reintroduce gratitude and ceremony into your daily life, welcoming the sun each morning and kissing her goodnight, and welcoming the moon rise, kissing her goodnight at dawn.

Shop local, shop small businesses, avoid big corporations. Filter your water from pesticides and fluoride. Minimize the 'products' you lather on your skin, the biggest, most absorbent organ in your body. Protect your gut from toxins in chemical-based foods and try to make and bake your own. Choose the simple slow life, prioritize rest and align yourself again with the circadian rhythms. Back farmers growing regenerative food with nature in mind; buy direct from them wherever you can. These are all suggestions for how we can reclaim our power and land, and restore balance and health back to our dying planet.

When working with any plant medicines always follow these three magic rules.

1. Thoroughly research the herb that is calling to you. Look in a trusted textbook or seek advice from a professional herbalist to give assurance and dosage; avoid online sites.

2. Ask if it's a safe herb with well-documented, tested usage.

3. Find out if the herb is safe for physical consumption, such as in a tea or tincture, or whether it is only for external use in a bath, smoke-cleaning ritual or shamanic-healing practice.

Hawthorn

One of my favourite medicines for keeping the heart in good shape is hawthorn. She has been used for centuries as a heart tonic and helps relieve palpitations, blood pressure, arrhythmias, cholesterol, circulation issues and physical manifestations of grief, such as heartache. Basically, if something is not functioning right within your cardiovascular system, she will set to working out the problem.

The rich antioxidants she contains help to protect our cells from harmful free radicals that put stress on our nervous systems.

Hawthorn trees are also known as May trees, because they bloom in May and the blooms and leaves can be used to make a tonic. Although the blooms can be made into an elixir (a tincture with honey added instead of alcohol), I tend to stick with the leaves and berries for a basic tincture. All the elements can make herbal tea when dried out and you can grind down the dried compounds to make capsules, jams and jellies, which set well because hawthorn is part of the apple family.

A RECIPE FOR HAWTHORN TONIC

To make a tonic, try to collect the fruits after frost or colder weather. This stimulates the tree to release more nutrients into the berries before winter shutdown.

Fill a Kilner jar with the berries – you can add the fresh leaves too – and cover them with vodka of at least 40 per cent proof.

Leave this for four to six weeks, then strain all the blood-red goodness and decant into small jars with pipets to take a few drops or a teaspoon daily.

This is not medical advice, so consult your doctor if taking any other medicines.

◇◇◇◇◇◇◇◇◇◇◇◇◇◇◇◇◇◇◇◇

Lemon balm

Lemon balm is a wonderous herb; earthy, bold and zesty. She is excellent for regulating women's hormones, particularly the thyroid hormones. Lemon balm is equally effective in the treatment of anxiety, as it takes the edge off the intense feelings of dread and nerves associated with anxiety. I recommend this herb in tincture form or as a tea.

RECIPES FOR LEMON BALM

Lemon Balm Tea

To make the tea, I collect bunches of lemon balm from my garden and leave them to dry for a few weeks, or put straight on to the dehydrator for a few hours. If you don't grow this herb, you can purchase dry organic lemon balm online.

Once dry, the plant can be crushed and put into a tea-making filter or metal ball and left to infuse in boiling water for a few minutes. Always add a little honey to taste as she can be on the bitter side.

Lemon Balm Tincture

To make a tincture, put the fresh or dry leaves into a Kilner or jam jar and fill with vodka or brandy that is at least 40 per cent proof. Completely cover the lemon balm, packing it down so that all plant matter is submerged.

Leave it for two to four weeks, then strain and bottle the liquid to take when required. A pipette full will suffice once or twice a day.

◇◇◇◇◇◇◇◇◇◇◇◇◇◇◇◇◇◇◇◇

Motherwort supports you during periods of emotional distress, especially related to motherhood and mothering. I also took motherwort to aid my healing from Graves' disease and regulate my thyroid hormones. Thyme is also a wonderful restorer of hope at the deepest level – something we all need while living through these times in our world.

The plants are our allies, our comfort and solace for times of restoration and healing. By learning the ways of our ancestors and the medicine they made, we honour those who were persecuted for practising such ways and killed for it. We keep their memory alive and rebuild that lost connection to nature and ourselves. On top of that, taking responsibility for our own health is one of the most radical and empowering things we can do for our self-worth and self-love.

CHAPTER 23

Gather

What the world needs now is everyday folk, people like me and you – individuals with fire in their bellies who can change the status quo. Have you ever thought about what legacy you will leave behind when you're gone? What will be your footprint upon this beautiful, magnificent home of ours? At the end of your life, will you be able to say, 'I made the most of it; I squeezed every last drop out of it, took every risk, seized each opportunity, embarked on many adventures.'? If you feel life slipping away and you're wasting time in a situation, job, house, environment or a relationship that's suffocating and depressing, then there really are only two choices: to stay as you are, the easy one; or to change, the hard one.

To face a spiritual challenge requires courage. Are you ready to find your true calling in this lifetime? Are you prepared to be refined and purified by the molten lava that courses through your veins and comes to awaken your spirit from a societal-induced coma that keeps you in a perpetual tame, conformist slumber? This path is not the easy one – it's for the bravest souls out there.

If you feel these words calling to you, and are ready to make that choice to move on to the next adventure in life, may I urge you, intentionally and courageously, to go in the direction of your heart and not your head. This quest is a venture into the darkness, the liminal space where your spirit likes to dance between the veils of humanity past and present to prepare you for the future. For spirituality is not born in the light, where we find enlightenment, but in the dark, where you'll unearth courage, your character and vision. So, never be afraid of the dark – the goddess of transformation is waiting for you there.

Creation story from the Hopi Nation, Arizona

The Creator said, 'I want to hide something from
the humans until they are ready for it.
It is the realization that they create their own reality.'
The eagle said, 'Give it to me. I will take it to the moon.'
The Creator said, 'No. One day they will go there and find it.'
The salmon said, 'I will bury it on the bottom of the ocean.'
The Creator said, 'No. They will go there, too.'
The buffalo said, 'I will bury it on the Great Plains.'
The Creator said, 'They will cut into the skin
of the earth and find it even there.'
Grandmother who lives in the breast of Mother Earth,
and who has no physical eyes but sees with spiritual eyes,
said, 'Put it inside of them.'
And the Creator said, 'It is done.'

Go in the direction of your heart and not your head. This quest is a venture into the darkness, the liminal space where your spirit likes to dance between the veils of humanity past and present to prepare you for the future.

To go through hardship and suffering in life feels almost like a rite of passage. Weathering storms and living a life of turbulence and rocky roads needs a good compass – the moon, cosmically connected to your solar plexus and soul. She knows life is full of uncertainty and is unpredictable. It's the nature of residing on a living, ever-evolving planet, where we have no control over our surroundings or destiny unless we shut ourselves in boxes, locking the world out and never interacting with communities or seeing sunrises, relying on machines to grow our food artificially. Oh, wait… that's now!

The battles I have faced in my life are nothing compared to the battle I have faced to live a free life on the land in the arms of Mother Nature. Women are the foundation of the community, a bedrock of steadfast resolve, desperate for peace and not war. We need access to our land again – the land stolen from us, the land that 'belongs' to no man. We are just keepers of our landscape, our farmland and meadows. We borrow the waters that sustain us and return it to the rivers. We are guardians of it all. But the distribution of our sacred land is so uneven among the population in this country that the poor, like myself, will always be fighting for scraps of it, like dogs over their last meal.

My ancient grandmothers were all nomadic, yours too. Life was harsh and brutal, as it is today, but they were free to roam, to find a spot by the river, near woodlands rich in foraging food, with animals to hunt, their feet and body always connected with the bare earth. They found medicine in the wild, heard the alarm calls of our animal relatives and spent every single night looking up at the stars, studying the cosmos and her patterns and cycles, and talking to the moon.

Think how different our life is now compared to our true origin and nature. In today's world, we can't even move through the landscape and camp along the way without being labelled vagrants and dossers, and booted off, punished for trespassing. Huge swathes of land and property are owned by wealthy individuals, establishments and organizations that lay claim to our remaining wild places, while we are herded like cattle into cities and made to pay for the privilege.

Yet despite knowing this – despite the hours, days, weeks and years spent pursuing a life sleeping on the earth – I cannot yet find a way for myself, my son and my flock to live on the land. So, for now, I rent from the rich and I borrow. And I manifest a place where women and children can come freely and be held by grandmothers, eat together, learn the crafts that will help provide for their families and build up a nation of warriors with blood-painted faces, ready to take back our Earth from the roots up. We will be backed by an army of trees, buffalo, sheep and wolves. This is the way to reclaim our Earth, bring freedom back to our children and restore balance.

Your purpose ignites a fire in your belly.

Your purpose is the whisper of your ancestors in the wind saying, 'This way, walk this way.'

You'll find you're gifted at it; that you'll bring others joy in this and that it makes you feel most at *home*. Your soul, spirit, body and mind are aligned in peace and passion, and when you find it, you'll dedicate the rest of your days to serving it.

Your purpose may evolve. It may take you to uncomfortable places and mean that you let go of people and dreams you thought were yours. But you'll learn to trust it. Let your intuition guide you, like a lighthouse in the storm.

Now, boldly and powerfully, go out into nature and lie down in a meadow, by the river or beneath a tall tree. Take off your shoes and feel the bare earth beneath your toes. Close your eyes, breathe deeply for several minutes and imagine you are surrounded by eagles hovering above you, waiting for the words to emerge from your mouth, to be caught and flown to where the Great Goddess, Mother Earth, resides. Speak out your heart: What troubles you? What do you long for? What grieves you? What truth do you want to see in your life? Finally ask her, if you feel so called, to use you. Your reason for being here right now, at this point in history, is by design and she is waiting for you to call out and give your life to this beautiful quest, to reconnecting with this beautiful planet we live on. See what comes out for you as you take a deep dive into your dream world.

Be the descendant who breaks the cycle.

Be the ancestor who left this legacy for your descendants.

Then, prepare for things to change. The signs and dreams will come. Then, be excited. Life's about to get *magical*!

Final Thoughts

I was born and grew up feeling like I was a nobody – or at least that's what the world told me. I lived in poverty and was always mocked for being the 'weird kid'; bullied for being unique or too deep. But I knew that deep inside me lay a magic lamp waiting to be rubbed. What emerged, through years of turmoil, suffering and being misunderstood, like the wolf, was a woman with a wild heart and a wolf by her side, who shall no longer be silenced.

I love all those things in me that society hated, and I am here to shine the same light on my fellow brothers and sisters; to tell them they *are* somebody, to remove the shackles of a corrupted world and fight for the one our ancestors worshipped and protected. For me, there is no greater purpose than to be a voice of truth for women at a time in history like we've never seen before. I agonized for so long over the feeling that I was born into the wrong time. This led me to a life of searching. I know now that I was born in exactly the right time, as are you. I was born to go out boldly into the world and capture every precious moment, feeling the fear of failure or anxiety, but doing it anyway. That's where the magic of life lies. The magic

I want to share wholeheartedly with the world, and I hope with all my heart that you will go out and share yours now, too.

Don't make the mistake of waiting for the right time. There is never a right time. As you take in your last breath and your heart beats its last drumbeat into the world, what will you be remembered for? And if you struggle to love people in this world, make trees the love of your life, or dogs, or the ocean or butterflies. I can assure you that they'll love you back and will be waiting for you when you cross over the rainbow bridge.

I want you to know I see you; I really do.

Remember your roots. Rediscover your origins. Reclaim your power.

May you never silence your voice.

May you never hide your magic or dim your light to fit in.

May you never be subservient.

May you walk through this world with the strength of the wolf... misunderstood but fiercely moving forwards with purpose and passion. May you never follow the flock.

Always...

... be a wolf, not a sheep.

Acknowledgements

To my son, Harry Richards, my constant inspiration in this world, for keeping my spirits up throughout this journey and always bringing light and laughter to my heart. I dedicate this book to you because you are – and always will be – my greatest inspiration and achievement. I have watched you grow into the incredible, strong man you have become, and now I can only hope you pursue a life full of adventure, purpose and as much happiness and joy as you bring me. But can you stop growing now, please!? Last count, 6ft 5in!

Aeyla, my wolfdog and greatest teacher! The three sheepdogs – Kes, the matriarch and once-in-a-lifetime companion, Skye, the sensitive but feisty princess, and Blu, the socially awkward loner.

Thank you, mother, for your passionate spirit and courage, my beating heart and keeping the magic alive through my lineage. I thank my father for my Irish fire and restless feet, my sisters, Amanda and Sophie, for being keepers of the Kneafsey strength and for encouraging my wildness, and I thank Stuart Moore (Mushtaguuuuuy! You get it.) – we are gonna be, forever, you and me; my rock and best friend.

I thank my stepdad, John Edwards, (Pops/Tramp) for being my reader and the calm in the storm, my dearest Wahiakeron – the Mohawk iron-worker and language-keeper and the English shepherdess (there's a film there, surely). How have I survived so long without you in my life, my love?! Keep sharing your wisdom and stories, the world needs you and there aren't many people who can say they've turned the Mafia down and are still here to tell the tale!

Kerry White, I absolutely couldn't have juggled all these animals, managed the sheep, dawgs, business and everything else, whilst writing a book, without you. Thank you.

I'm so grateful to Hay House for believing that I had this in me. Michelle, thank you for your patience, warm smile and encouragement. Thank you especially to my commissioning editor, beautiful Kezia – the reason I'm writing this. It's been a long road, but your unwavering support and belief that I could get to this point of sharing my heart with the world has been so humbling. It's an honour to work with you. Thank you, thank you. Lisa Lister, I'm soul grateful for you and your belief in my voice and heart.

Thank you to all the women who ever dared to be different and not follow the crowd. To the courageous ones who were afraid, but followed their potential and purpose and squeezed every last drop out of life! To the women who just *know* there's more to life than this – I see you and honour you with this book.

To Hannah Hauxwell, who is sadly no longer with us in this realm but whose spirit lives on in my heart. Thank you for being the role model I needed growing up – and still do now. Your resilience and passion for the land beneath our feet and the animals we share the Earth with has been a beacon of light in my life, and your memory and wistful nature drives me on. My heroine.

To Monica Sjöö, who influenced so much of this book and my transformational experiences. 'Take up the reigns,' she whispered to me as I read about her lifelong endeavour to strengthen the power of the feminine once more. She accompanied me through writing this whole book and, though she is also no longer on Earth, I hope she is smiling at me from the top of our beloved Silbury hill.

To the wolves for seeing me. To the moon for carrying me. To the flock... for ageing me well before my time.

Elizabeth Kneafsey

About the Author

Elizabeth Kneafsey, aka The Wild Wool Shepherdess, is a wild shepherd, wolf guardian, hide-tanner and wool witch who's been shortlisted for rural business awards and featured on TV and in magazines.

Elizabeth is passionate about supporting people with ancient discovery, simple ways of living, reclaiming their ancestral crafts, and wolf conservation. She runs a regenerative Shepherd's School, where she teaches animal husbandry and natural sheep care, and runs workshops on the ancient crafts of hide-tanning, fire-making and blade shearing. She sells her own wild-wool rugs, wool collars and organic sheepskins online and through her website. For every sale she makes, she gives a donation to the TreeSisters, who work with communities across the world to restore lost habitats *(www.treesisters.org)*.

In 2019, she was adopted into the Wolf Clan of the First Nation of the Kanienkeha'ka people, and became known as Iekawehatie *(yeah-ga-weh-ha-jay)*, 'she paddles along'.

 www.wildwoolshepherdess.com

 @wildwoolshepherdess

 @wildwoolshepherdess

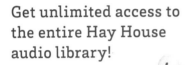

CONNECT WITH
HAY HOUSE
ONLINE

🌐 hayhouse.co.uk   **f** @hayhouse

📷 @hayhouseuk   𝕏 @hayhouseuk

▶ @hayhouseuk   ♪ @hayhouseuk

'*The gateways to wisdom and knowledge are always open.*'

Louise Hay